Webber

How to Build a College Fund for Your Child

PaineWebber

How to Build a College Fund for Your Child

Marion Buhagiar

A PERIGEE BOOK

This publication is designed to provide general information on the subject of financing your child's college education. This book is not a substitute for legal, accounting, tax, or other professional services. We recommend that a competent professional be consulted for answers to your specific questions. All information contained in this book is based on the current tax laws as of June 1989. The opinions expressed herein are not necessarily those of PaineWebber. While the information contained herein is believed to be accurate, it has not necessarily been independently verified by PaineWebber and is not guaranteed. Nothing herein should be construed as a solicitation or recommendation by PaineWebber with regard to the purchase or sale of any investment.

Perigee Books
are published by
The Putnam Publishing Group
200 Madison Avenue
New York, NY 10016

Library of Congress Cataloging-in-Publication Data

Buhagiar, Marion.
PaineWebber—how to build a college fund for your child.
Includes index.
1. Student aid—United States. 2. College costs—
United States. 3. Parents—United States—Finance,
Personal. 4. Investments—United States. I. Title.
LB2337.4.B84 1989 332.024 89-8401
ISBN 0-399-51534-8

Printed in the United States of America
1 2 3 4 5 6 7 8 9 10

Acknowledgments

First, of course, thanks to the many PaineWebber people who shared their expertise and advice to produce this book. I am especially indebted to Peter Hertz, who, at the onset of the project, enlisted their approval and assistance and to Gail Bliss, who, toward the end, coordinated their review of all chapters to assure accuracy.

Bertram J. Schaeffer, President of Philadelphia's Radnor Financial Consulting Group, Inc., which provides financial planning services for many PaineWebber clients, was generous and patient in sharing his expertise and experience to help me prepare the chapter on taxes and, most importantly, Part Two: "Making the Wisest Choices for Your College Fund." And I am indebted to Terri Smith, a certified financial planner with the same firm, for her unflagging diligence, courtesy, and good sense in also working with me on that section.

Dr. Frank Leana of Howard Greene Associates in New York candidly shared much of the wisdom he has gained over the past twenty years in counseling students about getting into college and their parents on how best to help them. Kalman Chany of New York's Campus Consultants was just as generous and wise in explaining the intricacies of the financial-aid process.

Patricia Robison and Roberta Romeo of Computing Independence in New York prepared many of the tables and projections in the book, always combining enthusiasm and good humor with their technical skills even as we worked late into the night. As a longtime editor myself, I am both admiring of and deeply grateful to Judy Linden, the editor of this book, for her energetic and skillful guidance on both big questions and small ones.

And finally, thanks to Alexa Ragozin, my daughter, who graduated from Brown University this year, who personally generated my interest in this subject, and who provided the best reason of all to do the book.

Contents

Introduction: Starting Right Now

You're very likely to freeze with anxiety when you look at a forecast of what it will cost to send your child to college fifteen or so years from now. Most everybody does. Next, you'll want to push the subject to the side "for now" and go on with the day's business, hoping that hard work, career success, and a little luck will solve the problem.

Actually, it may.

But since you cannot depend on luck alone, this book will enable you to take control of the situation. Your children, after all, deserve at least a little of the talent and energy you put into planning for your own success. If you can afford to save systematically, you'll need only a few hours *a year* to make the decisions necessary to assure your children that finances will not stand in the way of their getting the best education for which they're willing to strive.

Building up a college fund for your child can be more daunting than saving for a car, a big vacation, or even for the first down payment on a home. It is also probably the first—and only—substantial saving you will do for *someone else.* You've made a generous and mature decision to undertake the task—and with time on your side, common sense, and the practical advice in this book, you'll be successful. Enjoy the rewards.

PaineWebber

How to Build a College Fund for Your Child

I. THE NEW REALITIES

Use this part of the book to understand what is happening to college costs, what the tax and financial picture is now, and to work out a realistic savings program to meet your goal.

1

Can Families Really Afford It?

You're probably well aware of the inflation in medical-care costs in recent years. Well, the inflation in college costs has been far worse. In fact, tuition, room and board, and other fees at the nation's private universities have increased at a rate 30% greater than the increase in disposable personal income over the past decade.

The willingness of today's middle-income families to stretch their resources to send their children to college—and actually accelerate the demand for spots in the most costly elite schools—has surprised admissions departments all over the country. Two big factors are probably making that stretch possible for parents:

1. *The increase in the market value of their homes.* The incredible rise in real-estate values for those who purchased homes in the 1960s and 1970s has increased these homeowners' sense of personal wealth. And equity in their homes also provides them with an asset against which to borrow.

2. *The ability of women to enter (or reenter) the work force.* In many of these families, women have been a reserve source of earning power, providing income to maintain the family's chosen life-style despite the sudden outflow of cash when college expenses begin.

NO MORE WINDFALLS ON THE HORIZON

But these two sources of financial enrichment are not likely to be so available to new parents, and not-so-new parents, like yourself.

Real-estate values escalated so rapidly up through the mid-1980s largely because the baby-boom generation entered the market for housing. But over the next decade or so, the number of young adults in their mid-twenties to mid-thirties will decline. Demand for housing may soften and so, too, may the rate of real-estate appreciation in many areas of the country. Many parents of young children shouldn't count on tapping greatly increased wealth reserves in their homes in a decade or so.

Women are no longer an earnings reserve, either. Most mothers who are beginning to worry about the cost of college for their young children are already in the work force.

If this pattern fits you, it's clear that the major source of funding for your child's college education is going to have to be carved out of your family's income over the coming years. The earlier you start, the smaller that slice.

WILL TUITIONS KEEP CLIMBING?

You may be alarmed at the rate at which college tuitions have soared during the 1980s, but college-cost inflation has been running ahead of the level of general inflation in the U.S. for at least thirty years. Only when the general inflation rate hit double digits from 1972 to 1979 did college costs lag somewhat behind. Then, as general inflation dropped sharply, college costs stayed in an updraft. They're still going up at about double the overall consumer price increases.

There's nothing at all soothing in the tuition outlook, either. Some college administrators suggest that escalating tuitions in the 1980s were the result of faculty salary increases and essential maintenance that were deferred during the inflation of the 1970s. That might sound as though tuition increases could be modest from here on out. Unfortunately, this isn't likely. Demand for enrollment continues to be strongest at the nation's top colleges (which are often the most costly). That gives administrators very little economic incentive to make any serious effort to trim faculty size, additions to libraries and laboratories, or make any other cost cuts that could moderate tuition increases.

Tuitions were over $10,000 a year at 108 U.S. undergraduate colleges during the 1989 academic year. More than half the private four-year colleges in the U.S. billed the parents of their average student $7,700 to attend classes during that school year. College housing added about another $2,800–$3,600 a year, and books, supplies, transportation, and personal expenses added at least another $1,600. "No matter what the future price patterns of higher education," says Kathleen Brouder of the College Board, "it now ranks right up there with a home and well above a car as one of the largest purchases in most people's lives. As such, it deserves to be planned with at least as much care."

And that's just what you've started to do.

So, send in the coupon on page 192 for a very specific idea of what it will cost to send your child to college and what you'll need to save monthly to achieve that goal.

Meanwhile, for an inkling of what to expect in the future, say, the year 1999, review the three tables on pages 22 through 32. These summarize what's been happening—and what's likely to happen—to the cost of attending some of the nation's choicest schools, most of the state universities, and a random sample of additional schools.

The Fifty Schools with the Highest Tuition in 1989

The fifty four-year colleges with the highest tuitions during the 1988–89 academic year are in the table on page 22.

The average tuition at these schools was $12,965 for that year. And in the five years between 1985 and 1989, the average annual increase in tuitions was 8.5%.

In the two extreme right-hand columns, we have projected tuitions for the year 1999. This was done in two ways: (1) if the average annual increase at the school over the past five years continues to 1999; (2) if the average annual rate of increase is 7% a year (which is the long-term average rate for colleges).

Tuitions at these schools increased at the fastest average rate in 1987—9%. But in the two most recent years, the rate has been about 8.5%, indicating no significant downturn.

The schools with the highest average rates of increase during the past five years were Drew (up 11.7% a year, bringing its tuition from $7,210 in 1984 to $12,498 in 1989); Tulane (up 11.6% a year, bringing its tuition from $7,210 in 1984 to $12,730 in 1989); University of Chicago (up 10.6%, bringing its tuition from $8,043 in 1984 to

$13,285 in 1989); and Franklin and Marshall (also up 10.6%, bringing its tuition from $7,530 in 1984 to $12,460).

Among the schools in this group with the lowest rates of increase were Stanford (6.8% annually), Massachusetts Institute of Technology (6.9%), Bard (7.1%), and Harvard-Radcliffe and Princeton (both 7.2%).

ACTUAL 1989 AND PROJECTED 1999 ANNUAL TUITIONS AT FIFTY MOST EXPENSIVE FOUR-YEAR COLLEGES

COLLEGES	CURRENT TUITION 1989 ($)	ANNUAL INCREASE (%) 1985–89	PROJECTED 1999 TUITION	
			BASED ON 1985–89 RATE ($)	BASED ON 7% RATE ($)
AMHERST	13,105	8.0	28,390	25,780
BARD	13,560	7.1	26,925	26,675
BARNARD	12,918	7.7	27,041	25,412
BATES	13,920	9.4	34,192	27,383
BENNINGTON	15,670	7.8	33,333	30,825
BOSTON UNIVERSITY	12,975	9.0	30,842	25,524
BOWDOIN	12,565	7.6	26,153	24,717
BRANDEIS	13,066	8.4	29,203	25,703
BROWN	13,759	7.9	29,461	27,066
BUCKNELL	12,460	8.4	27,885	24,511
CARLETON	12,485	9.9	31,963	24,560
COLBY	12,620	8.7	29,007	24,825
COLGATE	12,350	8.1	26,836	24,294
COLUMBIA COLLEGE	12,878	7.6	26,752	25,333
CONNECTICUT COLLEGE	12,800	7.9	27,397	25,180
CORNELL	13,140	8.1	28,658	25,848
DARTMOUTH	13,335	7.8	28,369	26,232
DREW	12,498	11.7	37,710	24,585
FRANKLIN AND MARSHALL	12,460	10.6	34,148	24,511
HAMILTON	12,750	8.2	28,028	25,081
HAMPSHIRE	13,845	8.5	31,324	27,235
HARVARD AND RADCLIFFE	13,665	7.2	27,389	26,881
HAVERFORD	12,770	7.9	27,285	25,121

COLLEGES	CURRENT TUITION 1989 ($)	ANNUAL INCREASE (%) 1985–89	PROJECTED 1999 TUITION BASED ON 1985–89 RATE ($)	PROJECTED 1999 TUITION BASED ON 7% RATE ($)
HOBART	12,620	8.7	29,187	24,825
JOHNS HOPKINS	12,340	9.5	30,613	24,275
LEHIGH	12,450	9.2	30,155	24,491
MASSACHUSETTS INSTITUTE OF TECHNOLOGY	13,400	6.9	26,111	26,360
MOUNT HOLYOKE	12,940	8.2	28,417	25,455
OBERLIN	12,926	8.4	28,936	25,427
PITZER	12,986	8.3	28,924	25,545
PRINCETON	13,380	7.2	26,826	26,320
RENSSELAER POLYTECHNIC	12,600	7.9	27,069	24,786
SARAH LAWRENCE	13,280	7.3	26,765	26,124
SKIDMORE	12,440	8.8	28,894	24,471
STANFORD	12,564	6.8	24,346	24,715
SWARTHMORE	13,230	9.5	32,654	26,025
TRINITY	13,200	9.4	32,447	25,966
TUFTS	13,162	8.4	29,561	25,892
TULANE	12,730	11.6	38,210	25,042
UNIVERSITY OF CHICAGO	13,285	10.6	36,494	26,134
UNIVERSITY OF PENNSYLVANIA	12,750	7.5	26,290	25,081
UNIVERSITY OF SOUTHERN CALIFORNIA	12,466	9.6	31,277	24,523
VASSAR	12,490	8.4	27,895	24,570
WASHINGTON	12,574	9.6	31,463	24,735
WELLESLEY	12,580	7.8	26,740	24,747
WESLEYAN	13,325	8.6	30,491	26,212
WHEATON	12,370	7.8	26,147	24,334
WILLIAMS	12,975	8.5	29,409	25,524
WILLIAM SMITH	12,620	8.7	29,184	24,825
YALE	12,960	7.4	26,580	25,494
AVERAGES	12,965	8.5	29,388	25,504

Source of data for tables in Chapter 1: *The College Cost Book,* 1980–81, 1981–82, 1982–83, 1983–84, 1984–85, 1985–86, 1986–87, 1987–88, 1988–89 editions, copyright © 1980, 1981, 1982, 1983, 1984, 1985, 1986, 1987, 1988, College Entrance Examinations Board, New York. Reprinted with permission. Analysis and projections by Computing Independence, New York.

Tuitions and Projected Tuitions at Fifty State Universities

The table below lists the current and the projected tuitions for the year 1999 at fifty state universities.

During the academic year 1988–89, the average tuition at these schools was $1,776 and ranged from a low of $833 at the University of Wyoming to $3,440 at the University of Vermont.

Tuitions at these schools have been going up at an average annual rate of 8.1% over the past five years, with some schools well below that average (Kansas, Louisiana, Maine, New York, Oregon, and West Virginia) and some well above (Delaware, Hawaii, South Carolina, and the University of Texas).

Within the past five years, the highest annual tuition increases were made in 1985—an average of 11.5%. In the three most recent years, the average annual increases have been between 6.9% and 7.1%.

ACTUAL 1989 AND PROJECTED 1999 ANNUAL TUITIONS AT FIFTY STATE UNIVERSITIES

UNIVERSITIES	CURRENT TUITION 1989 ($)	ANNUAL INCREASE (%) 1985–89	PROJECTED 1999 TUITION	
			BASED ON 1985–89 RATE ($)	BASED ON 7% RATE ($)
ALASKA (FAIRBANKS)	1,250	9.8	3,187	2,459
ALABAMA	1,725	8.7	3,966	3,393
ARKANSAS	1,280	7.5	2,641	2,518
ARIZONA	1,278	8.6	2,909	2,514
CALIFORNIA (BERKELEY)	1,531	5.5	2,621	3,012
COLORADO (BOULDER)	1,860	9.3	4,534	3,659
CONNECTICUT	2,293	9.4	5,612	4,511
DELAWARE	2,790	15.4	11,677	5,488
FLORIDA	1,090	6.5	2,051	2,144
GEORGIA	1,839	8.2	4,051	3,618
HAWAII (MANOA)	1,227	14.3	4,667	2,414
IDAHO	1,042	5.2	1,735	2,050
ILLINOIS (URBANA)	2,398	9.4	5,904	4,717
INDIANA (BLOOMINGTON)	2,038	8.9	4,768	4,009
IOWA	1,706	9.1	4,090	3,356
KANSAS	1,325	4.4	2,038	2,606
KENTUCKY	1,412	6.8	2,733	2,778
LOUISIANA STATE (SHREVEPORT)	1,200	4.7	1,895	2,361

UNIVERSITIES	CURRENT TUITION 1989 ($)	ANNUAL INCREASE (%) 1985–89	PROJECTED 1999 TUITION BASED ON 1985–89 RATE ($)	PROJECTED 1999 TUITION BASED ON 7% RATE ($)
MAINE (ORONO)	1,630	1.2	1,843	3,206
MARYLAND (COLLEGE PARK)	1,740	5.9	3,076	3,423
MASSACHUSETTS (AMHERST)	2,400	7.9	5,144	4,721
MICHIGAN	2,900	7.6	6,043	5,705
MINNESOTA (TWIN CITIES)	2,163	7.4	4,429	4,255
MISSISSIPPI	1,780	6.9	3,456	3,502
MISSOURI (ROLLA)	1,918	6.5	3,588	3,773
MONTANA	1,351	10.5	3,663	2,658
NEBRASKA (LINCOLN)	1,693	8.6	3,873	3,330
NEVADA (LAS VEGAS)	1,200	5.4	2,040	2,361
NEW HAMPSHIRE	2,768	7.4	5,661	5,445
NEW JERSEY (RUTGERS)	2,744	10.4	7,398	5,398
NEW MEXICO	1,272	10.5	3,451	2,502
NEW YORK (ALBANY)	1,478	4.2	2,230	2,907
NORTH CAROLINA (GREENSBORO)	989	5.9	1,762	1,946
NORTH DAKOTA	1,472	7.7	3,102	2,896
OHIO (ATHENS)	2,394	7.3	4,823	4,709
OKLAHOMA	1,000	9.6	2,509	1,967
OREGON	1,556	2.4	1,982	3,061
PENNSYLVANIA STATE	3,126	8.1	6,824	6,149
RHODE ISLAND	2,331	6.1	4,199	4,585
SOUTH CAROLINA	2,230	13.8	8,088	4,387
SOUTH DAKOTA	1,708	6.6	3,237	3,360
TENNESSEE (KNOXVILLE)	1,404	10.5	3,809	2,762
TEXAS (ARLINGTON)	910	16.9	4,345	1,790
UTAH	1,644	9.6	4,117	3,234
VERMONT	3,440	5.7	5,991	6,767
VIRGINIA	2,526	12.8	8,440	4,969
WASHINGTON	1,797	9.1	4,295	3,535
WEST VIRGINIA	1,316	3.9	1,929	2,589
WISCONSIN (MADISON)	1,856	10.8	5,160	3,651
WYOMING	833	6.4	1,546	1,639
AVERAGES	1,777	8.1	4,063	3,496

Tuitions and Projected Tuitions at Other Top-Ranking Four-Year Schools

The colleges in the following table represent a broad selection of top-quality private four-year schools. The colleges are grouped by states. No average rates of increase are calculated for this group because it is a random selection.

ACTUAL 1989 AND PROJECTED 1999 TUITIONS AT TOP-RANKING FOUR-YEAR COLLEGES (ARRANGED BY STATE)

	COLLEGES	CURRENT TUITION 1989 ($)	ANNUAL INCREASE (%) 1985–89	PROJECTED 1999 TUITION BASED ON 1985–89 RATE ($)	PROJECTED 1999 TUITION BASED ON 7% RATE ($)
AL	AUBURN	1,323	6.1	2,384	2,603
	BIRMINGHAM-SOUTHERN	7,588	13.8	27,587	14,927
	SPRING HILL	7,700	8.9	18,144	15,147
AZ	ARIZONA STATE	1,278	8.6	2,909	2,514
CA	CALIFORNIA INSTITUTE OF TECHNOLOGY	11,789	6.1	21,296	23,191
	CALIFORNIA INSTITUTE OF ART	9,250	8.3	20,599	18,196
	CALIFORNIA POLYTECHNIC	870	15.1	3,560	1,711
	CHAPMAN	10,600	11.3	30,897	20,852
	CLAREMONT MCKENNA	11,870	8.2	26,080	23,350
	HARVEY MUDD	12,100	7.9	26,001	23,803
	MENLO	10,550	10.2	27,926	20,753
	MILLS	11,290	9.4	27,610	22,209
	OCCIDENTAL	12,078	8.9	28,267	23,759
	PEPPERDINE	12,115	10.0	31,539	23,832
	POMONA	12,000	8.2	26,381	23,606
	SANTA CLARA	8,784	9.4	21,575	17,279
	SCRIPPS	11,800	8.2	25,910	23,212
	UNIVERSITY OF THE PACIFIC	11,968	8.3	26,686	23,543
	UNIVERSITY OF REDLANDS	11,110	8.2	24,326	21,855
	WHITTIER	10,786	9.5	26,682	21,218
CO	COLORADO COLLEGE	10,240	7.9	21,989	20,144
	COLORADO STATE	1,800	7.7	3,762	3,541
	COLORADO SCHOOL OF MINES	3,475	6.4	6,443	6,836
DC	AMERICAN	10,480	8.2	23,030	20,616
	CATHOLIC UNIVERSITY	9,550	8.4	21,479	18,786
	GEORGE WASHINGTON	9,771	9.2	23,508	19,221
	GEORGETOWN	11,990	9.2	28,862	23,586
	HOWARD	5,005	13.4	17,594	9,846
FL	FLORIDA INSTITUTE OF TECHNOLOGY	6,201	10.7	17,156	12,198

	COLLEGES	CURRENT TUITION 1989 ($)	ANNUAL INCREASE (%) 1985–89	PROJECTED 1999 TUITION BASED ON 1985–89 RATE ($)	PROJECTED 1999 TUITION BASED ON 7% RATE ($)
	FLORIDA INTERNATIONAL	1,079	7.0	2,115	2,123
	FLORIDA STATE	1,100	5.7	1,923	2,164
	ROLLINS	10,881	10.9	30,733	21,405
	STETSON	7,675	10.1	20,127	15,098
	SOUTH FLORIDA	1,241	10.8	3,463	2,441
GA	BERRY	5,400	6.3	9,977	10,623
	EMORY	11,210	10.1	29,425	22,052
	GEORGIA INSTITUTE OF TECHNOLOGY	1,887	9.1	4,524	3,712
	MOREHOUSE	4,900	6.6	9,322	9,639
	OGLETHORPE	7,500	10.9	21,102	14,754
	SPELMAN	5,072	7.5	10,415	9,977
ID	COLLEGE OF IDAHO	8,032	10.5	21,750	15,800
IL	AUGUSTANA	7,848	8.6	17,920	15,438
	BLACKBURN	6,520	11.5	19,440	12,826
	BRADLEY	7,534	7.9	16,175	14,821
	DEPAUL	6,894	9.8	17,499	13,562
	ILLINOIS COLLEGE	5,000	8.8	11,636	9,836
	ILLINOIS INSTITUTE OF TECHNOLOGY	9,630	8.6	21,875	18,944
	LAKE FOREST	11,730	8.8	27,159	23,075
	NORTH CENTRAL	7,680	8.2	16,842	15,108
	NORTHWESTERN	12,270	6.7	23,361	24,137
	ROCKFORD	7,510	8.7	17,224	14,773
	SOUTHERN ILLINOIS (CARBONDALE)	1,903	7.9	4,061	3,743
	SOUTHERN ILLINOIS (EDWARDSVILLE)	1,595	6.3	2,940	3,138
	ILLINOIS (CHICAGO)	2,427	9.7	6,122	4,774
IN	WHEATON	7,728	7.9	16,595	15,202
	BUTLER	7,992	9.9	20,632	15,721
	DEPAUW	9,550	7.3	19,408	18,786
	EARLHAM	10,587	9.0	24,972	20,826
	GOSHEN	6,095	6.9	11,870	11,990
	HANOVER	5,330	7.0	10,488	10,485
	INDIANA (SOUTH BEND)	1,626	7.7	3,401	3,199
	PURDUE	1,854	5.4	3,145	3,647
	ROSE-HULMAN INSTITUTE	8,700	10.0	22,616	17,114
	ST. JOSEPH'S	7,260	10.4	19,456	14,282
	ST. MARY'S	8,479	7.9	18,079	16,679
	TAYLOR	7,694	9.6	19,216	15,135
	UNIVERSITY OF NOTRE DAME	10,472	9.9	27,021	20,600
	VALPARAISO	8,018	8.7	18,524	15,773

	COLLEGES	CURRENT TUITION 1989 ($)	ANNUAL INCREASE (%) 1985–89	PROJECTED 1999 TUITION	
				BASED ON 1985–89 RATE ($)	BASED ON 7% RATE ($)
	WABASH	8,200	7.2	16,465	16,131
IO	CENTRAL	7,410	7.8	15,660	14,577
	CORNELL	9,070	8.6	20,663	17,842
	IOWA STATE	1,706	9.1	4,090	3,356
	LORAS	6,840	8.8	15,826	13,455
	LUTHER	7,950	7.3	16,028	15,639
	WARTBURG	7,510	7.6	15,615	14,773
KS	KANSAS STATE	1,361	4.8	2,185	2,677
KY	BEREA	148	4.4	227	291
	CENTRE	8,050	6.2	14,693	15,836
	TRANSYLVANIA	7,750	6.3	14,340	15,245
LA	CENTENARY	5,540	9.3	13,538	10,898
	LOYOLA	6,819	11.3	19,844	13,414
MD	GOUCHER	10,165	7.4	20,718	19,996
	LOYOLA	8,005	12.0	24,785	15,747
	ST. JOHN'S	11,000	8.9	25,796	21,639
	WASHINGTON	9,600	12.6	31,361	18,885
	WESTERN MARYLAND	9,450	10.7	26,103	18,590
MA	BABSON	11,392	10.0	29,552	22,410
	BOSTON COLLEGE	11,076	9.6	27,581	21,788
	CLARK	12,170	9.2	29,377	23,940
	COLLEGE OF HOLY CRCSS	11,740	11.1	33,560	23,094
	EMERSON	10,275	9.2	24,687	20,212
	GORDON	8,870	9.2	21,451	17,449
	NEW ENGLAND CONSERVATORY OF MUSIC	10,850	8.8	25,218	21,344
	NORTHEASTERN	9,058	9.5	22,421	17,818
	PINE MANOR	10,700	8.3	23,707	21,049
	SIMMONS	11,028	8.5	25,022	21,694
	SIMON'S ROCK OF BARD	12,180	7.7	25,582	23,960
	SMITH	12,212	7.5	25,222	24,023
MI	ADRIAN	7,856	7.9	16,804	15,454
	ALBION	8,432	7.7	17,682	16,587
	ALMA	8,536	7.1	16,872	16,792
	CALVIN	6,180	7.6	12,891	12,157
	HOPE	7,930	8.0	17,042	15,600
	MICHIGAN STATE	2,546	8.2	5,590	5,008
	OAKLAND	1,716	4.8	2,750	3,376
	DETROIT	7,560	8.1	16,523	14,872
MN	BETHEL	7,800	9.5	19,377	15,344
	COLLEGE OF ST. CATHERINE	7,756	9.6	19,449	15,257
	COLLEGE OF ST. THOMAS	7,524	9.8	19,089	14,801

	COLLEGES	CURRENT TUITION 1989 ($)	ANNUAL INCREASE (%) 1985–89	PROJECTED 1999 TUITION BASED ON 1985–89 RATE ($)	BASED ON 7% RATE ($)
	CONCORDIA (MOREHEAD)	7,155	6.2	13,020	14,075
	CONCORDIA (ST. PAUL)	6,120	9.7	15,447	12,039
	GUSTAVUS ADOLPHUS	9,250	8.5	20,932	18,196
	MACALESTER	10,508	8.5	23,855	20,671
	ST. OLAF	9,165	8.6	20,886	18,029
	MINNESOTA (DULUTH)	2,105	4.2	3,189	4,141
MS	MILLSAPS	7,385	9.7	18,641	14,527
MO	ROCKHURST	6,480	8.7	14,927	12,747
	ST. LOUIS	7,090	7.3	14,319	13,947
	WESTMINSTER	6,550	6.9	12,729	12,885
	WILLIAM JEWELL	6,140	10.0	15,964	12,078
NE	NEBRASKA WESLEYAN	6,488	7.8	13,735	12,763
NH	COLBY-SAWYER	9,980	7.5	20,550	19,632
NJ	STEVENS INSTITUTE	12,025	10.8	33,522	23,655
NM	ST. JOHN'S	11,200	9.3	27,194	22,032
NY	CANISIUS	6,830	8.1	14,881	13,436
	CLARKSON	10,665	7.7	22,468	20,980
	COOPER UNION	300	−19.3	35	590
	EASTMAN SCHOOL OF MUSIC	11,400	6.8	22,059	22,426
	FORDHAM	8,525	8.8	19,857	16,770
	HOUGHTON	6,874	9.4	16,878	13,522
	LEMOYNE	7,000	8.3	15,567	13,770
	MANHATTAN	7,450	9.8	18,934	14,655
	NEW YORK	12,250	11.2	35,497	24,098
	POLYTECHNIC	11,180	9.5	27,788	21,993
	PRATT	9,122	8.7	20,955	17,944
	ST. LAWRENCE	12,300	9.3	29,842	24,196
	SIENA	6,890	8.2	15,203	13,554
	STATE UNIVERSITY (BINGHAMTON)	1,515	5.6	2,614	2,980
	STATE UNIVERSITY (BUFFALO)	1,465	5.9	2,592	2,882
	STATE UNIVERSITY (STONY BROOK)	1,495	5.7	2,613	2,941
	UNION	12,313	8.6	28,025	24,222
	UNIVERSITY OF ROCHESTER	12,305	9.4	30,113	24,206
	WELLS	10,410	6.4	19,412	20,478
NC	DAVIDSON	10,235	12.2	32,314	20,134
	DUKE	12,286	11.8	37,423	24,168
	GUILFORD	7,910	10.7	21,762	15,560
	NORTH CAROLINA STATE	896	5.7	1,554	1,763

	COLLEGES	CURRENT TUITION 1989 ($)	ANNUAL INCREASE (%) 1985–89	PROJECTED 1999 TUITION BASED ON 1985–89 RATE ($)	PROJECTED 1999 TUITION BASED ON 7% RATE ($)
	UNIVERSITY OF NORTH CAROLINA (CHAPEL HILL)	845	3.8	1,229	1,662
	WAKE FOREST	7,950	9.5	19,707	15,639
	WARREN WILSON	6,650	8.9	15,608	13,082
OH	ANTIOCH	10,460	10.1	27,360	20,576
	CAPITAL	8,700	8.2	19,114	17,114
	CASE WESTERN RESERVE	11,000	8.6	25,001	21,639
	CLEVELAND INSTITUTE OF MUSIC	9,046	5.7	15,737	17,795
	DENISON	11,360	8.6	25,857	22,347
	JOHN CARROLL	6,784	9.4	16,624	13,345
	KENYON	11,840	8.4	26,587	23,291
	MIAMI (OXFORD)	3,026	7.9	6,460	5,953
	MOUNT UNION	9,320	7.1	18,421	18,334
	MUSKINGUM	9,380	9.3	22,741	18,452
	OHIO NORTHERN	8,385	10.9	23,537	16,495
	OHIO STATE (COLUMBUS)	2,040	7.1	4,069	4,013
	OHIO WESLEYAN	10,076	8.2	22,248	19,821
	UNIVERSITY OF CINCINNATI	2,532	8.7	5,820	4,981
	WITTENBERG	10,702	8.6	24,402	21,052
	UNIVERSITY OF DAYTON	6,920	9.8	17,676	13,613
	XAVIER	7,000	8.8	16,223	13,770
OK	OKLAHOMA STATE	1,050	10.4	2,830	2,066
	ORAL ROBERTS	5,075	6.7	9,670	9,983
OR	OREGON STATE	1,506	2.1	1,861	2,963
	LEWIS AND CLARK	10,401	8.4	23,207	20,460
	REED	11,350	8.6	25,886	22,327
	WILLAMETTE	9,480	9.6	23,789	18,649
PA	ALBRIGHT	9,935	9.6	24,770	19,544
	ALLEGHENY	10,425	10.0	26,992	20,508
	BRYN MAWR	12,155	7.5	24,977	23,911
	CARNEGIE MELLON	12,080	9.9	30,962	23,763
	DICKINSON	12,230	9.9	31,383	24,058
	DREXEL	8,916	11.3	26,118	17,539
	GETTYSBURG	12,200	11.6	36,489	23,999
	INDIANA UNIVERSITY OF PENNSYLVANIA	2,054	4.5	3,181	4,041
	JUNIATA	9,540	9.8	24,246	18,767
	LAFAYETTE	12,025	9.3	29,160	23,655
	MESSIAH	6,750	8.6	15,465	13,278
	MORAVIAN	9,880	9.5	24,507	19,435
	MUHLENBERG	11,720	12.3	37,230	23,055

	COLLEGES	CURRENT TUITION 1989 ($)	ANNUAL INCREASE (%) 1985–89	PROJECTED 1999 TUITION BASED ON 1985–89 RATE ($)	PROJECTED 1999 TUITION BASED ON 7% RATE ($)
	UNIVERSITY OF PITTSBURGH	3,810	8.7	8,749	7,495
	UNIVERSITY OF SCRANTON	7,184	13.0	24,477	14,132
	URSINUS	9,000	9.9	23,229	17,704
	WESTMINSTER	7,700	7.0	15,112	15,147
	WILSON	8,774	7.7	18,393	17,260
RI	RHODE ISLAND SCHOOL OF DESIGN	11,350	8.6	25,808	22,327
SC	CLEMSON	2,090	5.2	3,478	4,111
	FURMAN	8,100	10.9	22,803	15,934
	WOFFORD	7,135	9.2	17,270	14,036
SD	AUGUSTANA	7,345	7.1	14,569	14,449
TE	CHRISTIAN BROTHERS	5,790	9.6	14,446	11,390
	UNIVERSITY OF THE SOUTH	11,050	9.0	26,140	21,737
	VANDERBILT	11,975	11.0	34,081	23,557
TX	ABILENE CHRISTIAN	4,440	9.6	11,104	8,734
	AUSTIN	7,250	9.4	17,760	14,262
	BAYLOR	4,720	8.8	11,008	9,285
	RICE	5,525	7.2	11,115	10,869
	SOUTHERN METHODIST	9,064	7.6	18,845	17,830
	SOUTHWESTERN	6,950	10.1	18,204	13,672
	TEXAS A & M	1,060	18.5	5,781	2,085
	TEXAS CHRISTIAN	6,536	7.2	13,040	12,857
	TEXAS TECH	911	16.1	4,070	1,792
	TRINITY	8,160	11.8	24,973	16,052
	UNIVERSITY OF DALLAS	6,450	9.9	16,538	12,688
	UNIVERSITY OF HOUSTON	950	18.3	5,112	1,869
	UNIVERSITY OF TEXAS (AUSTIN)	862	18.0	4,514	1,696
	UNIVERSITY OF TEXAS (DALLAS)	870	12.9	2,926	1,711
UT	BRIGHAM YOUNG	1,720	5.1	2,834	3,384
VT	MARLBORO	12,200	9.6	30,619	23,999
VA	COLLEGE OF WILLIAM & MARY	2,966	11.0	8,430	5,835
	GEORGE MASON	1,824	5.8	3,203	3,588
	HAMPDEN-SYDNEY	9,530	7.9	20,366	18,747
	HOLLINS	9,200	7.0	18,061	18,098
	JAMES MADISON	2,702	10.4	7,293	5,315
	MARY BALDWIN	7,750	8.1	16,892	15,245
	MARY WASHINGTON	2,264	13.7	8,172	4,454
	RANDOLPH-MACON	8,425	8.9	19,772	16,573

	COLLEGES	CURRENT TUITION 1989 ($)	ANNUAL INCREASE (%) 1985–89	PROJECTED 1999 TUITION	
				BASED ON 1985–89 RATE ($)	BASED ON 7% RATE ($)
	RANDOLPH-MACON WOMAN'S	9,410	7.4	19,258	18,511
	SWEET BRIAR	10,140	6.9	19,678	19,947
	UNIVERSITY OF RICHMOND	9,080	8.2	20,019	17,862
	VIRGINIA POLYTECHNIC	2,544	13.0	8,608	5,004
	WASHINGTON AND LEE	9,005	9.0	21,235	17,714
WA	EVERGREEN STATE	1,318	5.5	2,262	2,593
	GONZAGA	8,300	9.4	20,393	16,327
	PACIFIC LUTHERAN	8,520	9.9	21,947	16,760
	UNIVERSITY OF PUGET SOUND	9,100	8.9	21,302	17,901
	WESTERN WASHINGTON	1,344	5.9	2,395	2,644
	WHITWORTH	8,415	8.5	19,076	16,554
WI	BELOIT	10,004	7.2	20,120	19,679
	CARROLL	8,600	7.2	17,216	16,918
	LAWRENCE	10,770	8.5	24,281	21,186
	MARQUETTE	6,984	7.5	14,453	13,739
	RIPON	10,267	9.1	24,641	20,197
	ST. NORBERT	7,690	9.7	19,483	15,127
	WISCONSIN (MILWAUKEE)	1,915	10.8	5,362	3,767

HOW MUCH IS COLLEGE WORTH, AFTER ALL?

In the 1970s, the declining value of a college education in the American economy was the subject of much public and private concern, and taxi drivers with Ph.D.'s were a running joke. Economist Richard Freeman even examined the subject in great detail in his book, *The Overeducated American,* which demonstrated that a 54% earnings advantage in 1971 for college graduates over high-school graduates with five years of work experience was down to only 40% in 1974. By 1979, that difference probably narrowed to 35%. Far more rapidly than anyone anticipated (including Dr. Freeman, as he's quick to admit), the value of a college education made a comeback.

If you graduated from college at the end of the 1970s, statistics projected that you could expect to take seventeen years to recoup in earnings the expense of four years at a public college and four years of lost earnings. By now, that "payback" time has shrunk to about eleven years—despite the accelerating increase of college costs during the 1980s.

There are, of course, further benefits to that college degree. The college-educated are much less likely to be laid off, unemployed, or partially employed. And they certainly get first chance at the best jobs, working under the best conditions.

The gap in earnings between the "haves" (employees with a college degree) and the "have-nots" (employees whose education stopped at high school) is widening sharply. By 1986, those with a college degree earned 80% more than those with just a high-school diploma during the first five years of work following graduation, according to a study by economists Kevin Murphy, of the University of Chicago, and Finis Welch, of the University of California, Los Angeles.

It's reasonable to expect the advantages enjoyed by the haves to be even greater by the time your child is ready for college. Eminent management consultant Peter Drucker is already warning his major corporate clients that they may soon be operating in a world where half the U.S. work force is made up of college-educated "knowledge workers," while "the other half" could become a serious social concern because their lack of education blocks them from ways to move up economically.

The chief reason for the widening gap is not so much what is going on in the executive suites and professional offices to which college graduates aspire. Rather, it is the sharp erosion of high-paying (usually unionized) jobs for high-school graduates in heavy industry. Given the lower birth rates during the 1960s, the number of young men and women looking for jobs right after graduating from high school is already down 16%, and "Help Wanted" signs paper the windows and doors of many fast-food restaurants, retail stores, and banks. Those jobs, however, usually have very low wage horizons.

Giving your child the college edge is likely to be one of the best investments you ever make—and it's certainly a lot more satisfying than most.

HOW MUCH FINANCIAL AID TO COUNT ON

Federally supported aid for college students declined by about 10% in real dollars (adjusted for inflation) during the first half of the 1980s.

Only about 15% of the college freshmen during the 1989 academic year reported receiving federal grants—well under half the proportion who received such grants in 1980. "Since 1980, the federal government has dismantled most of the financial aid programs intended to assist college students from middle-income families," reports the Higher Education Research Institute of the University of California, Los Angeles. Even federal loan programs, which had begun to replace grants, are drying up. Don't plan on a major expansion of aid or federal-backed loans in the foreseeable future, despite the pro-education rhetoric in Washington. You'd be more realistic to count on an austere climate for such assistance over the next decade, until the federal deficit is brought down significantly. Most federal aid to students at private colleges can easily be attacked as support for the "privileged" at the expense of the many since it is primarily the children of the relatively well-off who attend those schools.

And it won't matter much whether inflation or recession marks the years ahead. Inflation would increase the federal government's interest costs—and threaten the entire educational-aid program. Recession would reduce revenues and increase pressures for social welfare spending—again at the expense of aid to students going to private colleges.

(Part Four of this book, "The Means to Be Successful," summarizes the current situation and the trends in financial aid.)

NEW BOOSTS TO COLLEGE SAVING

A revenue-hungry Congress has already choked off some of the most long-standing and best tax-advantaged ways to build college funds. Middle- and upper-income families traditionally saved for college by shifting assets into trusts and custodial accounts for their children. The use of these techniques is now much more restricted. (See Chapter Three, "The Few Tax Advantages Left for College Saving," page 46.)

Both Congress and the states, however, appear to be far more willing to encourage parents to save to meet future college tuitions than to increase financial aid. The income on Series EE savings bonds bought from January 1, 1990 on will be free of federal, state, and local taxes if redeemed to pay college tuition and fees by parents whose income doesn't exceed a certain level. (See Chapter Eleven, "U.S.

Savings Bonds: A Whole New Twist to an Old Way to Save for College," page 125.)

States, too, are trying to come to the rescue with various tax-advantaged programs to encourage college savings because they have great voter appeal. By early 1989, fifteen states had approved ways for parents to use special educational savings accounts and local and state tax-free bonds to meet tuition expenses. (For details, see page 179.) But a recession is likely to leave many states in a vulnerable financial condition. In 1988, state and local governments ran a record deficit of $14.4 billion, the second year in a row they ran significantly in the red. Public colleges and universities are, of course, already subsidized by state tax revenues. During recessions, enrollments at these lower-cost public schools usually spurt, putting even greater pressure on state budgets.

IN OTHER WORDS, YOU'RE ON YOUR OWN

There's no government-supported rescue boat in sight for you. If you want to assure yourself that your child will get at least as good a college education as you had, you'll have to find ways to save out of current income and invest it wisely.

Fortunately, financial institutions have been extremely creative in recent years about devising investment products to meet a variety of needs. The variety may seem confusing—but you'll find it less so once you review the selection guidelines, based on your child's age, in Part II of this book.

You'll have to take the measure of the task, figure out what you can realistically save, and then invest appropriately. The next chapter explains how to use this book step-by-step to reach your goal.

2

The New Frugality: How to Use This Book for Your College Savings Plan

You're well on your way to making your own college savings plan. Just use the special step-by-step guides prepared by the experts in college investing who put this book together.

Throughout this book you'll find two levels of help:

1. Expert information on the most effective investments for college fund building—how they work, ways to buy them, how to measure performance.

2. Specific guides so that you can personalize this information and apply it to your family's special needs—the age of your children, your income level, your tolerance for risk.

Whatever decisions you make by applying these personal guidelines will be a great deal more effective than impulsively responding to the promises in an advertisement or a sales pitch, shopping with no special direction among the confusing array of investment choices now available, or doing nothing at all.

More likely, you'll be surprised at your success, because disciplined, long-term investing gives you a great deal of power.

You can start saving even with a very general goal of what you will eventually need. Tuition at the state universities may average about $4,000 a year in a decade, for instance. By that time, the average tuition at one of the fifty highest-tuition schools is likely to be more than $25,000 a year. Add to that an estimate for room and board, books, transportation, and a living allowance for each child.

If you have specific schools in mind, check the lists that begin on page 22, which project 1999 tuitions at more than three hundred top schools. Sending in the coupon on page 192 will get you not only the projected costs at a particular school for your child when he reaches 18, but also four model savings plans to reach that specific goal. You could purchase *The College Cost Book 1988–89,* ($12.95), which contains current expense information on over three thousand U.S. colleges and universities, from your local bookstore or directly from the College Board, 45 Columbus Avenue, New York, NY 10023-6992. You can also call the school or schools you have in mind, find out the current tuition, ask how much those costs have been going up annually for the last few years, and prepare your own estimate.

This book will then guide you, step by step, to work out a personal plan to meet the goal you've set for yourself. But the follow-through is up to you. Even managers of multimillion-dollar corporations, aided by hundreds of MBAs and millions of dollars' worth of computers, are generally uncomfortable planning more than three years ahead, which you'll have to do.

Their solution is one you can easily adopt. Don't simply make a plan and consider the problem solved. (Those plans usually wind up in a desk drawer, unused, even in big companies.) Instead, consider college savings to be a rolling plan. That's a project you review and alter, if necessary, every year or so, depending on results (looking back) and changes in needs (looking ahead).

To start your college-savings rolling plan, you need:

1. An estimate of the college expenses you're likely to face.

2. Realistic thinking about saving, including a tough assessment of your family's ability to set aside money for a college fund.

3. A guide to selecting the most appropriate investments for your college fund so you can focus your search knowledgeably.

4. A good understanding of the pros and cons of the basic investments you'll probably consider so that you make sound decisions.

You'll find the information and guidelines you need for each of these tasks in this book.

THE COLLEGE EXPENSE YOU'LL FACE

Send in the special coupon at the end of the book for a personalized college savings plan and you'll soon have a forecast of what college is likely to cost for your child and how much you'll have to save month by month to reach that goal.

Essentially, you should anticipate college-cost inflation of about 7% a year—the average annual rate of increase in college costs over the past thirty years. The range of annual tuition increases from school to school is quite wide, however. The Ivy League schools have generally been going up at an average rate of between 7% and 8% a year since the mid-1980s. Duke University, however, has been going up at an average rate of 11.8% during that time. The rate of increase has been more modest at most big state universities, but the University of Wisconsin at Madison, for instance, has been going up at 10.8% in that same period.

Suppose, for example, you graduated from Duke University in 1971 (when tuition was $2,100 a year) and you would like your 3-year-old boy to have the same opportunity in fifteen years or so. If Duke's tuition continues to increase at an 11.8% rate, it will cost you over $65,000 a year by then—well above what is projected for Harvard and Yale by that time. Even if the annual rate of increase at Duke goes down to about 7% in the years ahead, you'll be facing an annual bill for tuition alone that could be close to $34,000—or $136,000 for four years of undergraduate work. (Tuition and fees at Duke amounted to $12,286 for the 1989 academic year.)

Or perhaps you'd like to think that your bright 5-year-old daughter deserves a chance at Yale, Harvard, or Princeton in thirteen years. Tuition there will likely be about $33,000 a year.

Your 11-year-old is showing every sign of being able to compete for the best, too, and you'd like him to be able to consider Brown or Swarthmore, both of which will then be around $24,000 a year if their tuitions continue to escalate as they have during the past five years.

You graduated in 1973 from Bryn Mawr (tuition then $2,800 a year) and your husband from Haverford the same year (tuition $2,760), and you'll encourage your 1-year-old and 3-year-old girls to think about going to top-notch smaller colleges too. Bryn Mawr's,

Haverford's, and Reed's current cost-inflation rates could bring their tuitions up to over $40,000 a year by 2006. Carleton College in Minnesota would be over $62,000 a year by then if it continued its 9.9% annual rate of increase; bringing its cost escalation down to 7% would take Carleton to the $40,000-a-year range by the year 2006.

And even though state universities are subsidized by taxpayers, tuitions there, too, have been increasing over 8% a year during the 1980s. By the time your 4-year-old is ready to consider one of them, Michigan could be up to $8,000 a year, Wisconsin to $9,000, and UCLA to over $3,000 a year.

REALISTIC THINKING ABOUT HOW MUCH YOU CAN SAVE

If you haven't saved much in recent years, you're not alone. Americans are notoriously bad savers. For a generation or so, they've "saved" chiefly by investing in their homes or piling up profit-sharing and pension benefits on the job. But the fact that you are reading this book is just one of many strong indicators that the tide is shifting.

Given the rate of college-cost inflation, even dual-paycheck families with fairly substantial incomes and good earnings prospects take a big risk by assuming they'll be able to meet college bills out of what they'll be earning when their children are ready for college and what they "managc to put asidc" now. Mccting hcavy collcgc costs and maintaining a top-quality life-style during the years in which those expenses are concentrated and assuring yourself an adequate retirement income simply can't be done casually.

You really have no other choice but to save cash, to attempt to increase the rate at which you save, and to dedicate a portion of that saving to building a college fund. Here's an old rule of thumb for the New Frugality: Save 10% of total income (salaries before taxes plus all investment income for a dual-income family with two children and no extraordinary expenses for medical care, handicapped family members, or aged parents to support). Many financial planners suggest a rate of at least 15% if the family income ranges between $75,000 and $125,000 a year, 20% if income ranges between $125,000 and $200,000, and more than 20% for those earning above $200,000. Another dedicated savers' rule: Save the entire take-home pay of one working spouse.

Building your college fund is doomed to failure if you limit yourself to saving "what's left over." For your savings plan to work, your monthly check to a savings account has to assume the same priority as those you make out for the mortgage, car payments, utilities, and the phone and cable TV bills.

Here's how to figure out what you're currently saving:

1. Look at your year-end statements for last year and the year before and figure out if there was an increase in the cash balances of your checking, savings, money-market accounts, or asset-management accounts at your brokerage firm.

2. *Add* to that figure (if it's positive) the money you put last year into certificates of deposit, stocks, bonds, or other investments, including IRA contributions or cash additions to a Keogh or other self-employed retirement plan.

3. *Add* the amount you personally contributed to company profit-sharing, retirement, 401(k), and other savings plans. Optional: Add the sum your employer contributed to such plans during the year. That was money added to your annual income that you didn't spend, so technically it is savings. (Remember, though, that only the part of your employer's contribution that is fully vested is yours for sure.)

4. *Add* the amount of principal you paid off on your mortgage—and the down payment on a house, if you made one last year.

5. *Add* the increase in cash value on insurance policies, if you owned any.

6. *Add* a figure for repaid debts if you trimmed the amount outstanding on credit cards at the end of the year compared to the year before, if you paid off a loan, or if you reduced the principal outstanding on a car loan.

7. *Subtract* the amount of any loans you took out during the year (including any increase in credit-card balances due compared to one year ago), investments you cashed in, or money you withdrew from a company savings plan.

The total is what you saved—in dollars—during the year.

YOUR SAVINGS WORKSHEET

1. Increase (or decrease) in cash balances of your checking accounts, savings accounts, money-market accounts, and asset-management accounts between year ago and now $________

2. Money added during the past 12 months to
   - CDs $________
   - IRAs $________
   - self-employed retirement plans $________
   - stock purchases $________
   - bond purchases $________
   - other investments $________

   Total $________ + $________

3. Money you personally added during the past 12 months to company
   - 401(k) plan $________
   - pension plan $________
   - profit-sharing $________

   Total $________ + $________

4. (Optional) Money your employer added to such plans during the past 12 months.
   - 401(k) plan $________
   - pension plan $________
   - profit-sharing $________

   Total $________ + $________

5. Principal paid off on mortgage during the past 12 months or down payment on a home + $______

6. Increase in cash value of life insurance policies during the past 12 months + $______

7. Repaid debts during the past 12 months, including
   - reduced credit-card balances $______
   - repaid loans $______
   - reduced principal on car loan $______

   Total $______ + $______

8. Loans taken out during the past 12 months, including
   - increased credit-card balances $______
   - investments cashed in $______
   - withdrawal from company savings plans $______
   - personal loans $______

   Total $______ − $______

Total saved over the past 12 months $______

To determine your rate of savings last year:

1. Total your income from all sources during the year (except loans and credit)—including wages and salaries, your contributions to company savings and retirement plans (and your employer's contributions, if you want to consider them), and interest and dividends on your savings and investments.

2. If you make substantial payments to a cash-value life insurance policy, add the total increase in cash value for the year plus dividends and subtract the amount of premiums you paid during the year. This net amount is an increase in savings.

3. Total these figures to arrive at your total earned income for the year. Then divide your total savings figure for the year (say, it amounted to $5,000) by total income (say, it totals $60,000) to arrive at your savings rate (5,000 divided by 60,000 = 8.3%).

Now, when you receive your personalized college savings plan or make a rough estimate of what college expenses are likely to be for your child, you'll be able to see how your current savings level compares to what you'll probably need to save to finance your child's education at the school you've selected.

If you come up short, don't despair. Take a hard look at your family's savings rate and discuss ways to adjust it upward. And remember, this is a rolling plan. Save what you can, and your regular review of investment results and cost projections may yield some pleasant surprises in the years ahead. Furthermore, though you shouldn't count on financial aid in your planning because there's no way to forecast its availability, your child may qualify for aid or some form of subsidized loan program when the time comes. What you've managed to save by then, however, may make all the difference to your child's choice of school.

SELECTING THE MOST APPROPRIATE INVESTMENTS FOR YOUR COLLEGE FUND

In Part Two of this book, "Making the Wisest Choices for Your College Fund," you'll find a simple but systematic way to match your own family's needs with the most appropriate investment alternatives. The key factor here is the age of your child. So, start by using the Contents to find the pages covering your child's age. There you'll find a quick summary of the kinds of investments you should consider first—as well as the ones you probably should not consider.

On these pages there are also several examples of specific investment choices recommended by PaineWebber financial-planning experts for families with varying incomes and children of different ages.

Investment choices are ranked by risk to give you a clear idea of what alternatives you can choose from to strike a balance between your need to preserve the capital in the college fund and your drive to build it up. You can use the information you gain by reviewing these choices to work with an investment executive at PaineWebber, or with another trusted financial adviser, to develop a personalized plan based on your special needs.

UNDERSTANDING THE PROS AND CONS OF INVESTMENT ALTERNATIVES

For help in making sound choices of where to put your college-fund savings, you'll move to Part Three. There you can review the pros and cons of all the investments PaineWebber experts consider appropriate for a college fund.

Remember, you don't have to decide on everything all at once. Your first task is to lay down a conservative base—a solid foundation—with funds you've already saved for this purpose or the money you'll start to set aside this year. Then review your options regularly. As the time when you'll be sending your child off to college draws closer, keep reviewing the personal guide in Part Two to alert you to the need to shift money from one kind of investment to another so that you enhance your chances of realizing your goal safely.

But always . . .

- Think long term. If you switch and trade the wealth you're building up in your college savings program too often, you could wind up with less money than if you concentrate on capital conservation and long-term results.
- Make sure you don't underestimate your own family's potential needs for cash in the years ahead. In your eagerness to save for college, be careful not to sacrifice too much liquidity—that is, assets you can turn into cash quickly during both good markets and bad. In general, maintain a cash reserve of at least half a year's expenses outside of any custodial accounts or trusts for your child. (If you lock up assets in a trust or custodial account, you can't access those funds for your personal expenses.) Keep in mind another conservative rule of thumb:

A person who loses a job should be prepared to take an average of one month for every $10,000 of salary to find a new one. Without an adequate cash cushion, you might be faced with a cash emergency that forces you to sell one of the investments in your college fund before you had planned. If you do that too often, your savings plan will go off track. Your investment results are very likely to suffer also because you might have to sell shares, bonds, or funds at just the wrong time in the market, taking a capital loss when holding on would have produced a gain.

3

The Few Tax Advantages Left for College Saving

Before launching into the hard work of saving for college, you should be clear about the major ways to avoid taxes on the wealth you'll be accumulating and earmarking for college expenses.

You're working in an entirely different environment from that enjoyed by the upper-income families of previous generations of college-bound children who were able to set up plans that pared taxes to the minimum on funds slated for college tuition. Prior to the major overhaul of federal tax laws in 1986, parents easily reduced taxes by shifting cash or income-earning property into short-term trusts, especially so-called Clifford Trusts, which allowed the trust assets to revert to parents after ten years. This income shifting took earnings out of the parents' high tax brackets and put it into the lower brackets of their children. Under former tax laws, parents were also able to fully deduct interest paid on student loans, which is no longer possible.

There's an ironic advantage to this development. You now can concentrate on making the soundest investment decisions for your college fund instead of worrying chiefly about taxes. Making tax savings the key factor in deciding how to invest your money is rarely wise. Many investors, for instance, still find themselves trapped in tax shelters that produce "losses" (largely the result of high depreciation deductions) that, under current tax law, no longer can be used to offset their investment income or high salaries or professional fees. By focusing only on taxes, you might also put substantial assets beyond your control—in the hands of your child when he or she reaches the age of majority—and then find the money isn't used for college at all, or for any other purpose you wanted to encourage.

To put the tax burden on your college fund into perspective, remember that federal income tax rates are generally lower now than they were when parents put so much effort into income shifting. But rates may not stay so low in the years to come. That means you have to stay flexible.

Congress, for instance, has now expanded the opportunity for tax-free saving to meet college expenses through the use of Series EE savings bonds. The benefit, available for the first time in January 1990, is limited, however, to families with low and moderate incomes (see page 125). State legislatures are developing tax-advantaged savings plans also, many of them designed to encourage parents to send their children to state colleges and universities.

Though tax-saving devices for college savings are sparser under current laws, what's available now is easy to understand and use. However, before adopting any of the following strategies, be sure to consult your tax adviser.

THE ADVANTAGES OF SHIFTING

To make sound decisions, you need to know what you can achieve now by income shifting. The basic limitation under current federal income-tax law is the so-called "kiddie tax." The kiddie tax applies to the investment income of a child who has not reached the age of 14 before the end of the year. In general, the first $500 of that child's unearned income is reduced by his $500 standard deduction. The next $500 of such income is taxed at the child's tax bracket—typically 15%. All of the child's unearned income in excess of $1,000 is then taxed at either the child's marginal tax rate or that of the parents (usually 28% or 33%), whichever is highest. The year a child turns 14, *all* the child's unearned income begins to be taxed at his or her tax bracket.

Basic tax-saving opportunity for children under 14 years of age: Limit the taxable investment income earned in the child's custodial account to $1,000. Tax-free municipal bonds or zero municipal bonds are useful. So are Series EE savings bonds purchased for the child by a custodian, because interest that accrues on these bonds can be deferred until the bonds mature or are redeemed. If the bonds mature or are redeemed after your child reaches 14 years of age, the kiddie tax on that income is avoided. (Of course, the interest on these bonds will be tax-free if used to pay tuition for your children, *if* you buy them in your own name starting January 1, 1990, *and* you meet the income limitations described in Chapter Eleven.)

If that $1,000 of income is included in your return and is taxed at 33%, you'll give the IRS $330 of the earnings each year. With the income in your child's name, however, the total federal income tax is only $75 a year (no tax on the first $500 and 15% on the remaining $500).

That's a $255-a-year tax saving, which may seem negligible unless you consider how it can contribute to your college fund. Investing $255 after-tax each year at 8% a year compounded adds over $8,600 to your savings in seventeen years.

Tax planning for building a college fund involves two tax issues: Shifting income to the lower tax bracket of your child or placing it in a trust fund for your child *and* avoiding federal gift taxes. In order to shift income, you must transfer assets to your child or to a trust. The first $10,000 gift made by you as an individual to each child during the calendar year is excluded from federal gift taxes and no gift tax report need be filed with the IRS. A married couple can each make a $10,000 gift to a child (a total of $20,000 a year) without filing a gift tax return. Or one spouse can make a $20,000 gift and file a gift tax return showing that the other spouse consents to the gift. (The tuition you pay for your child's education is not considered a taxable gift.)

If you decide for personal reasons not to shift assets to your child *before* he or she is 14 years old, you can still arrange to shift substantial sums when the child reaches that age to take advantage of his presumably lower tax bracket at that time:

1. Use extended-family planning. Both parents can contribute to the child—bringing the gift-tax-free sum for a year up to $20,000. Add a grandparent, and it's $30,000. Another grandparent, and it's $40,000. Meanwhile, the funds will have been part of the family's general assets, giving you more financial flexibility. Keeping it in your hands until then also allows you to adapt to future changes in the tax law.

2. Transfer to your 14-year-old child securities on which you have a significant paper profit or an appreciated real-estate investment that you're ready to contribute to the college fund. Then, when the securities or real estate is sold, the gain will be taxed at the child's lower rate instead of your higher one.

You might also consider a universal life-insurance policy on your life that is owned by your child (or by your parent, who makes a gift every year of the insurance premiums), particularly if you decide life insurance is necessary to fund education costs in the event of your premature death. As long as certain guidelines are met, the buildup of cash in these life-insurance policies will not be subject to current income taxes. If you die prematurely, the policy's proceeds will go directly to your child tax-free. If you survive, the policy can then be surrendered and the income realized when the child is 14 years old or older. Or you might borrow against the investment in the insurance contract to fund education costs without incurring taxes, when IRS conditions are satisfied.

Much more important than these tax-saving techniques, however, are your own priorities. You can minimize taxes also, of course, by simply investing your college fund in tax-advantaged municipal bonds or, starting in 1990, in Series EE savings bonds. You might be able to increase your yield, however, by transferring taxable assets to your child. But the cost is losing control over those assets.

Another consideration is financial aid. You have no way of knowing what rules will apply by the time your child is ready for college. Right now, if the family qualifies for any tuition support package, $350 of every $1,000 saved in a child's name but less than $60 of every $1,000 of savings in the parents' name will be considered available for tuition. For that reason, some financial-aid counselors recommend moving funds out of the child's name as college approaches.

WOULD YOU RATHER SEPARATE THE COLLEGE FUND FROM OTHER ASSETS?

Obviously, these are not all cool, abstract, bottom-line decisions. So, while you're pondering how much you trust your child as well as potential tax savings, also do some hard, realistic thinking about how you save best.

Many people are more likely to save consistently in a segregated account dedicated to a specific goal. That alone—aside from any tax-saving considerations—could be a good enough reason to build up most of your child's college fund in her own name. Also, money put aside in your child's name is out of the reach of your creditors' claims.

MAKING YOUR CHILD A TRUST-FUND BABY

The most common form of making gifts to minor children is under the Uniform Gifts to Minors Act (UGMA) or the Uniform Transfers to Minors Act (UTMA), which the majority of states have adopted. Gifts to minors under these acts qualify for the $10,000 annual federal gift-tax exclusion.

A brokerage firm or a bank will give you the appropriate application form to set up such an account, and no special fees are usually charged. The "name" on the account will be long, listing both the name of your child and the custodian. Your child's Social Security number identifies the account. All dividends and interest paid on shares, bonds, or cash held in a custodial account are paid to the custodian of the account. The account funds must be used for the exclusive benefit of the child. You cannot simply terminate the account and withdraw the assets to use them for some other purpose if you subsequently change your mind. When your child comes of age, assets in the custodial account are his or her property entirely and you will not be able to control how they are used.

You should not act as the custodian of the account if you are the donor of the assets in the account. Custodial account property will be included in your estate for federal estate tax purposes if you are both the donor and act as custodian at the time of your death. A spouse who is *not* a donor, however, can be a custodian of the account without running this risk.

The UGMA or UTMA custodian account is completely different from a bank account (or any other account) in your name "in trust for" your child, which has no special tax-saving features. The Social Security number on such an account is yours, income is fully taxable to you, and you can use the funds for any purpose and close out the account whenever you wish.

The kind of assets you can accumulate in custodial accounts is generally governed by whether your state follows the Uniform Gifts to Minors Act (UGMA) or the Uniform Transfers to Minors Act (UTMA).

In general, the revised (1986) Uniform Gifts to Minors Act permits investments in custodial accounts of securities, cash, bank accounts, credit-union accounts, savings-and-loan accounts, mineral interests, and life insurance. It does *not* generally permit investments in real property or partnership interests, though some states that follow the UGMA include them.

The Uniform Transfers to Minors Act (UTMA) generally permits investments in custodial accounts of more types of property, including real property, life insurance, and partnership interests.

For a modest fee of about $500, a lawyer familiar with trust matters can set up a simple trust that can avoid the kiddie tax but not taxes altogether.

The most common is the so-called Minors Trust, formally known as a 2503(c) Minors Trust, which generally provides that the trust fund (income and principal) be used for the benefit of the minor. All funds remaining in the trust must be distributed to the child when he or she reaches the age of 21.

The trust itself pays income taxes on income accumulated by the trust and not distributed to your child. At present, the first $5,200 of undistributed trust income is taxed at 15%. Any income above that is taxed at a 28% or 33% bracket. Your benefit: If that $5,200 were added to your family income, it most likely would be taxed at the 28% or 33% rate.

By setting aside funds for your child in such a trust, you're in a position to shift about $6,000 of annual income into the very lowest tax brackets, giving a substantial lift to the return on your college savings fund. Here's how it would work with a trust earning $6,000 a year (8%) on $75,000 in assets:

- The trust could pay out $1,000 of its investment income directly to your child. If that is your child's only unearned income, he would be liable for $75 in federal tax (at the 15% tax bracket). The remaining $925 could be invested in tax-free municipal bonds in his name. If that $1,000 was earned by a college fund in your name, you would probably pay federal tax at the 33% rate—$330. So $255 a year goes back to work generating money for college rather than to the IRS. (As noted above, that's over $8,600 if invested at 8% compounded for seventeen years.)
- The remaining $5,000 of income generated by the trust that year would stay in the trust to be taxed at only 15%, or $750. If that

income were taxed at the family's top bracket of 33%, the IRS would take $1,650. That's a tax saving of $900 a year under the current tax law. Invest that $900 at 8% compounded annually after tax instead of sending it to the IRS and you've added an additional $30,075 to your college fund over seventeen years.

Assuming no change in the tax law, using this trust would add over $38,000 to your college fund over seventeen years simply through tax savings. Your costs: Fees to set up the trust and to file estimated tax payments and an annual income tax return for the trust.

Before you're dazzled by these prospects, a reminder that when you put assets in a trust or custodial account, you lose control over those assets when your child comes of age.

Distribution of the trust assets to your child can be delayed beyond age 21 if he or she is given a reasonable time to withdraw assets from the trust upon reaching that age. Even if your 21-year-old does not withdraw the assets then, all trust income will be taxed to him or her from that point on, not to the trust on the trust's tax rate.

If you are not comfortable with giving your child the right to receive what may be substantial trust assets at age 21, you can consider a Crummey Trust. The major advantage of such a trust is that distribution of trust assets can be delayed to any age you choose.

A Crummey Trust can be created for anyone at any age, but for college-fund tax planning, it is established for your minor children. The trust contains a provision giving your child power for a period of time (at least thirty days) to withdraw gifts or asset transfers you make each year to the trust. If the child does not withdraw the funds, they become part of the trust, to be administered according to its own provisions.

Special income-tax rules apply to Crummey Trusts. Be sure to get qualified legal advice if you consider setting one up.

In all states, parents are under a legal obligation to support their minor children. In many states, higher education is considered a support obligation if the parent has adequate funds. In general, income from a custodial account or 2503(c) Minors Trust used to discharge the legal obligation of the parent *will be taxable to the parent.* So, if higher education is considered a support obligation under the laws of your state, be sure to consult with your tax adviser before setting up a custodial account or trust. Approaches to avoid the possible tax consequences are sometimes possible.

Every dollar that goes toward your child's education rather than to the IRS is going to give you great satisfaction. But consistent saving and intelligent investing are far more important to the achievement of your goal than tax avoidance. Perseverance is entirely in your hands. In Part Two, which follows, you'll find the guidelines you need to make sound investment decisions now and in the years ahead with the cash you do set aside for your child's future.

II.
MAKING THE WISEST CHOICES FOR YOUR COLLEGE FUND

Use this section of the book to select the investments most suitable for the special needs of your family's college fund, based on your child's age and your tolerance for risk.

4

Risk and Time: The Key Factors in Making the Most of Your Savings

The obvious advantage of starting your college fund when your child is young is that you have more time to accumulate savings and put the power of compounding to work. Equally important is the investment flexibility you gain during the early years of your savings plan.

The longer your lead time to the day you write your first tuition check, the more risk you can afford to take to increase the earnings rate on your college fund. Most people shy away from risks and are willing to pay the cost in exchange for greater certainty that they are preserving their capital. In fact, studies by behavioral scientists show that, even when the odds are 50-50, most people will bet only if they see a chance to win *twice* as much as they can lose. The pain of losing is simply too great to enable them to play the odds by cool calculation.

Certainly, your approach to investing for your child's education should always be fairly conservative. With time on your side, however, you can at least consider stock funds—even aggressive-growth stocks—and real-estate investments that often provide excellent opportunities for long-term wealth building but can also be subject to sharp ups and downs along the way. You can invest in longer-term bonds when interest rates on those bonds are much more attractive than those on shorter-term issues because you can hold the bonds to maturity and cash them in when your child is in college without worrying about any fall in the market value of the bonds along the way. If interest rates go up during that period, you can invest new savings in shorter-term issues at even higher rates. You can ride out the typical four- to six-year cycles of the stock market, taking, and thus preserving, your profits in an up-market well before you *must* liquidate your holdings because you need the cash for college.

Just having a great deal of choice, however, doesn't mean that it always makes sense to scatter your savings among a variety of investments. Some of the most successful professional long-term investors, who can afford to invest millions of dollars at a time, keep their portfolios down to ten or fewer issues at a time. You need only enough variety to spread your risk by diversifying. Nor does the fact that you *can* take more risk mean that you're wrong to stay in investments geared more to preserving capital than generating a high rate of return. You should *never* put the savings in your college fund into anything that makes you feel uncomfortable just because some experts say you can afford to take the risk.

The other advantage of making a long-term savings plan and sticking with it is that your college fund is far less likely to be buffeted and damaged by sharp, short-term swings in interest rates in the securities markets, or in the economy. You're far less vulnerable to following the herd—buying when the market is high and selling when it's down—if you take the time to understand what you're doing and why, and follow your chosen guidelines.

As you investigate the ways you can invest your savings:

• Never—never!—invest in anything you don't fully understand. Ask to have the risks (there are always some) explained to you as well as the potential profits.

• Be sure you understand how liquid the investment is—what penalties there might be for cashing it in before a certain time.

• Don't rush into a variety of investments just because you're anxious to get started, especially if you've been used to keeping most of your savings in CDs or money-market funds. By focusing on a few alternatives, you can be thoughtful about each choice, compare the rewards it promises against alternatives—and monitor actual performance against expectations.

In the chapter that follows, you'll find College-Fund Investment Selection Guides, prepared with the help of PaineWebber's financial planning experts. The Guides are arranged by child(ren)'s age and by risk, giving you a quick way to review the alternatives that suit you best.

5

College-Fund Investment Selection Guides

The single most important factor in the appropriateness of an investment for your college fund is the number of years you have before you must cash it in to meet college expenses. Once your child is accepted by a college, you'll begin to cash in investments and withdraw funds. You'll liquidate the fund in a fairly short period of time—four to five years. You don't want to be at the mercy of a weak market for any of your investments during that time.

For that reason, the Investment Selection Guides in this chapter are arranged so you can quickly refer to the information appropriate to the age of your child, which determines the number of years you have left to save for college. Ages are indicated at the beginning of each section.

You can turn directly to the page with your child's age for the information you need now about building up your college fund. Investments appropriate for your current savings are arranged there by risk level. The least risky (which usually means you can expect to earn less on these selections) are listed first, followed by those with a higher risk (and higher expected earnings rates). No highly speculative investments are included in these Guides, since PaineWebber considers them inappropriate for educational funding.

The Guides can also help you develop a relationship with an investment expert you trust, who understands and respects your long-term goals and who is informed enough to help you think through alternatives. Use the Guides to focus your attention. This way you're likely to do a more responsible job of investing for your child's future than if you simply "tracked the market" every day, or tried to read every bit of financial and business news. Resist impulsive decisions. And on tax and legal matters, consult a professional.

If you're an Early Planner, read those pages of this section carefully, of course, but also look further along in the chapter to the Investment Guides for parents of older children. They will give you an idea of what you should think about to manage your fund effectively in later years.

In Part Three you will find specific information on how to assess and buy each of the investment alternatives listed in the following Investment Selection Guides.

EARLY PLANNERS

College-Fund Investment Selection Guide
(Child's age: 1–6)

Least risk
Savings accounts
Money-market funds
Certificates of deposit
Treasury bills
U.S. savings bonds
U.S. government bonds, including zero bonds, if held to maturity
CollegeSure CD

Little risk
Investment-grade corporate bonds (rated Baa or higher) and unit investment trusts of these bonds held to maturity
Investment-grade or insured municipal bonds and unit investment trusts of these bonds held to maturity

Moderate risk
Government securities mutual funds
Investment-grade corporate-bond mutual funds
Municipal-bond mutual funds
Convertible bonds and preferred stock
Balanced, growth-income, and growth mutual funds
Common stocks of major companies with seasoned earnings and dividend performance records.
Real Estate Investment Trusts

Higher risk
Common stocks of smaller companies
Aggressive-growth and growth mutual funds
Global- and international-equity mutual funds
Global- and international-fixed-income mutual funds
High-yield (junk) bond mutual funds
Real-estate limited partnerships

Strategy

With a cushion of twelve years or more before college-fund investments have to be cashed in to meet school expenses, long-term and somewhat illiquid investments, such as real estate partnerships, can be tolerated.

Volatility in a security—that is, a tendency for the price to swing sharply up and down—is a severe risk if you know you must liquidate the investment within a few years, because the year you need the cash may turn out to be at the low end of the market cycle. The Early Planner's time cushion significantly reduces this risk. So, those of you starting to build your college funds while your children are young can consider aggressive-growth funds, global funds (which invest in shares of companies around the world), and the stocks of fast-growing companies. These investments are generally more volatile but might contribute to producing a higher overall rate of growth than a portfolio made up solely of balanced funds and stocks of well-established companies with long, steady earnings and dividend records.

Of course, just because you are an Early Planner, there's no reason to accept even this risk if it makes you uncomfortable.

College-Fund Savings Plans: Examples for Early Planners with Young Children

Chris and Roberta Romeo have two children, Ann, 2, and Rudy, 4. Their combined gross income is about $75,000 a year. In addition to their emergency cash reserve of $15,000, they have $10,000 set aside for a college fund for their children. The Romeos are in the 28% tax bracket in 1989, but, based on their estimate of future compensation hikes, they will probably be in the 33% bracket in two years.

The Romeos' current cash flow enables them to save at least $9,500 each year toward future college expenses. They are planning to buy a larger home, however, in the next couple of years and expect their monthly mortgage payments to increase. They worry that the higher monthly expense might put them under too much financial pressure to maintain the savings goal, though they would make every effort to do so. They are also uncomfortable with the idea of establishing Uniform Gifts to Minors Act (UGMA) accounts for their children.

The Romeos are prepared to take only moderate risk to reach their goal—affording a "name" private four-year college for both Ann and Rudy.

They decide to invest their $10,000 college fund in:

Short-term municipal-bond unit investment trust	$4,000
Intermediate-term municipal-bond unit investment trust	$4,000
Balanced equity mutual fund	$2,000

The Romeos have established a college fund oriented toward producing income. Although they do not intend to dip into the college fund for income, they are more comfortable knowing that the income would be there when they incur higher mortgage expense in the future.

The municipal-bond unit investment trusts provide tax-exempt current income, which avoids tax at their 28% bracket level now and possibly higher rates in the years ahead. The maturities in these municipal-bond UITs are staggered from short- to intermediate-term, which provides a hedge against the risk of higher interest rates in future years. If interest rates do go up, the Romeos would be able to reinvest the proceeds of the maturing short-term UIT at the higher rates.

The balanced equity mutual fund, which invests in bonds, preferred stocks, and common stocks, provides good current income and modest potential for long-term growth. Thus, it meets their investment objectives of generating income *and* preserving capital. In future years, once the Romeos reassess their cash flow and their ability to save additional money in their college fund, they could consider a regular monthly investment in a growth equity mutual fund.

If the Romeos continue to save $9,500 a year for their children's college fund and earn an average after-tax return of 8%, they will have $254,000 in their fund by 2003, which is likely to be enough to send both Ann and Rudy through fine schools such as Cal Tech, Wellesley, Southern Methodist, Rice, or Hollins.

Patricia and James Glass have a 1-year-old child, Robert, and a combined gross annual income of $100,000. Their marginal federal tax bracket in 1989 is 33% and they feel confident that their cash flow (income less expenses) will remain good.

The Glasses have a cash reserve of $25,000 for emergencies and have already saved an additional $9,000 toward a college fund for Robert. Putting the "save 10% of gross" guideline to work, they now expect to save another $10,000 this year—and at least that amount in future years.

All their savings are currently in a money-market fund. But Pat and Jim are ready to take some risk in return for the prospect of a higher return.

Because of the size of the Glasses' investment portfolio ($34,000), they have decided not to establish a UGMA custodial account for Robert. They decide, however, to earmark $19,000 of the total for Robert's college fund and invest in:

High-grade, zero-coupon municipal bond (matures at $35,000 in 2006)	$10,000
Growth equity mutual fund	$4,500
Aggressive-growth equity mutual fund	$4,500

What have the Glasses accomplished? The zero-coupon municipal bond gives them the certainty of $35,000 available in 2006, when Robert is 18 years old. The growing value of the bond as the interest accrues will be exempt from federal income tax.

With seventeen years to go until Robert's first year of college, the Glasses have a long investment time horizon and can accept the volatility associated with both the growth and aggressive-growth equity mutual funds. So, for the near term, they expect to keep investing equal amounts of their monthly college-fund savings in the two mutual funds. Depending on how tax laws develop over the years and the Glasses' own feelings about giving up ownership of their assets, they could make a gift of the equity mutual funds to a UGMA custodial account for Robert in the future. If the funds appreciate, the custodian of the account could sell the fund shares once Robert was at least 14 years old and the gain would then be taxed at Robert's own, presumably lower, tax rate.

If the Glasses achieve an annual return of at least 10% after-tax a year on their college fund, and if they continue to put aside $10,000 a year from 1989 until 1994, they will have what they expect to need (about $198,000) for Robert to go to an Ivy League school well *ahead* of the time he's ready to apply.

Maddie and Tom Thomson also have two children, aged 3 (Mark) and 4 (David). They have a substantial combined income of between $150,000 and $175,000 a year and a $75,000 portfolio at their brokerage firm. Both have a low tolerance for risk. They neither like to be actively involved themselves in managing their college fund nor do they want it actively managed by anybody else. They're happiest making a few solid decisions a year and buying to hold.

The Thomsons are in the 33% federal tax bracket. Their projected cash flow is excellent and they anticipate being able to contribute $20,000 to $25,000 a year to a college fund for the next seven to eight years. They hope the boys will be able to qualify for Ivy League schools. All looks well for the Thomsons to build a college fund of the size they need so long as both work. But they have begun to review their insurance coverage and have become concerned about what might happen to their plans in the event of Tom's premature death. So, they decide that part of their college-fund investment strategy should include additional insurance on Tom's life.

The Thomsons decide to establish separate UGMA accounts for Mark and David, with a close friend acting as custodian of the accounts. Tom makes a gift of $12,000 to each of the accounts, which is within the $20,000 split-gift annual exclusion but they will have to file a gift tax return that year. The custodian of the boys' accounts will apply for a universal life insurance policy on Tom's life in the face amount of $100,000 for each account. The estimated annual premium is about $800 for each policy. Based on the dividend record of the insurance company and conservative interest-rate assumptions, each policy could have a cash value of $16,400 in fourteen years.

The Thomsons decide to invest the remaining $11,200 in each account in:

Zero-coupon U.S. Treasury bond (matures at $25,000 in 2003)	$7,100
Growth equity mutual fund	$4,100

What have the Thomsons accomplished? The universal life insurance policy assures a basic sum available for Mark and David in the event of Tom's premature death. Because the custodian is the owner and the one who applied for the insurance, the proceeds will not be included in either Tom's or Maddie's estate for federal estate-tax purposes.

The cash value of the universal life policy will build up tax-free. If Tom survives, when the children reach college age, the custodian can either surrender the policy (triggering some income tax) or borrow against the investment in the insurance contract (deferring taxes and continuing the policy).

The annual accretion of interest on the zero-coupon U.S. Treasury bond (about $650 a year) will be income to each child. Since this is less than $1,000 a year in unearned income, it avoids the kiddie tax under the current tax law.

If the Thomsons save $20,000 for education purposes each year for the next seven to eight years, and if the investments achieve an after-year annual rate of return of 7% between now and 2003, they will probably have enough—close to $350,000—to finance their two boys through Ivy League schools.

EARLY PLANNERS

College-Fund Investment Selection Guide (Child's Age: 7–12)

Least risk
Savings accounts
Money-market funds
Certificates of deposit
Treasury bills
U.S. savings bonds
U.S. government bonds, including zero Treasuries, if held to maturity
CollegeSure CD

Little risk
Investment-grade corporate bonds (rated Baa or higher) and unit investment trusts of these bonds held to maturity
Investment-grade or insured municipal bonds and unit investment trusts of these bonds held to maturity

Moderate risk
Government securities mutual funds
Investment-grade corporate-bond mutual funds

Municipal-bond mutual funds
Convertible bonds and preferred stock
Balanced, growth-income, and growth mutual funds
Common stocks of major companies with seasoned earnings and dividend performance records
Real estate investment trusts

Higher risk
Common stocks of smaller companies
Aggressive-growth and growth mutual funds
Global- and international-equity mutual funds
Global- and international-fixed-income mutual funds
High-yield (junk bond) mutual funds
Real-estate limited partnerships

Strategy

Your investment options are virtually the same as for Early Planners with younger children *except* that your investment time horizon is shorter. Liquidity takes on added significance. Real-estate partnerships that project that they will liquidate properties in eight to ten years may no longer be appropriate investments for new savings. Long-term bonds or unit investment trusts of bonds with fifteen- to twenty-year maturities extend beyond the years when you will probably have a maximum need for cash to pay college expenses. If you had no other substantial cash resources at that time, you would face the risk of having to sell those bonds or UITs at an unfavorable time in the market cycle. The way to minimize your risk is to structure a college fund with long-term investments scheduled to mature *during* the years your child expects to be at college.

College-Fund Savings Plans for Early Planners with Older Children

Mary and Frank Pietrzak have two children, Alexa, 7, and Adam, 9. They have a fund for emergency expenses and have also saved $15,000 toward college expenses for the children. Out of their combined gross income of $55,000 a year, the Pietrzaks figure they can continue to put away $6,300 a year for this purpose. All their savings are currently invested in bank certificates of deposit and a money-market fund.

The Pietrzaks, who are in the 28% federal tax bracket, want to retain ownership of their investments. They're willing to take moderate risk with the funds earmarked for college expenses, with the goal of being able to send their children to first-rate state universities—or better.

They decide to invest their $15,000 college fund in a family of funds:

Growth equity mutual fund	$5,000
Growth-income mutual fund	$5,000
Municipal-bond mutual fund	$5,000

Each month the Pietrzaks intend to invest $525 in approximately equal amounts among the funds and reinvest all dividends, interest, and capital gain distributions back into the funds.

The Pietrzaks have put together a diversified college fund with above-average potential for long-term growth and the risk of only moderate price volatility. Although they have no investments that will mature at a given date to provide a specific sum (such as a bond), historical rates of return suggest that the Pietrzaks can expect their investments to grow faster than the inflation rate. With nine years to go until Adam attends college, their investment time horizon is sufficiently long to allow them to get through the average up-and-down volatility to which their portfolio will be subject.

The systematic $525-per-month savings put into a family of funds will give the Pietrzaks the advantages of dollar-cost averaging—investing the same fixed amount at regular intervals. They will accumulate more shares in months when the funds' share prices are low and less shares when the funds' share prices are high. Over time, with this strategy, their average cost per share will be less than the average price of all their share purchases.

If the Pietrzaks manage to achieve an after-tax return of 8% on their college fund, they will have almost $109,000 in 1988 when Adam is ready for college. Even though tuition at state universities is going up an average of 8% a year, a college fund that size will probably be enough to finance both children through the best of them, debt-free, and with ample funds to meet living expenses and out-of-state fees.

Judy and Bruce Manalapan have a 7-year-old boy, Peter, with a mathematical and scientific bent. If Peter chooses and qualifies for

MIT or Rensselaer, they want to make it financially possible for him to go to one of those schools.

The Manalapans have a combined gross income of $90,000 a year. They've been consistent savers, so they have about $20,000 set aside to meet college expenses—most of it in CDs. They estimate that they can add $11,000 a year to their college fund and are willing to assume modest investment risk. In addition, Judy's parents have indicated a willingness to contribute to their grandson's college expenses. The Manalapans, who are in the 33% federal income-tax bracket, decide to establish a UGMA account for Peter with a close friend acting as custodian. Bruce will make a gift of $20,000 to the account. In order to avoid gift taxes, they will file a gift tax return on which Judy will consent to the gift thereby availing themselves of the $20,000 annual gift tax exclusion. Judy's parents also will make a $20,000 gift to the same UGMA account and likewise file a gift tax return.

The Manalapans decide to invest the $40,000 college fund in:

CollegeSure CD (assume purchase 3/31/89, variable interest rate averaging 9% a year, maturity value estimated at $39,000 in 2000)	$15,000
Real-estate limited partnership (expected to liquidate in eight to 10 years)	$7,500
Growth equity mutual fund	$8,800
International equity mutual fund	$8,700

The Manalapans have put together a growth portfolio with inflation protection and tax advantages. The CollegeSure CD provides some protection against the inflation of college costs because the interest credited to this special CD account increases in relation to increases in college expenses (see Chapter Seven for a further explanation). The interest on the CollegeSure CD will constitute unearned income to Peter. At the current rate, the CD's annual income is $1,350 a year. The first $1,000 will avoid the kiddie tax.

The real-estate limited partnership is a low-leveraged partnership which projects annual cash distributions of 6% on the Manalapans' investment during the first few years and an increase to 8% in later years. Of the 6%, only 3% is projected to be taxable because of the shelter of depreciation deductions.

The partnership anticipates selling its properties in eight to twelve years and liquidating the partnership. By that time, Peter will be 15 to 19 years old. All income realized on the liquidation will be taxable to him at his tax bracket. In addition to the current cash distributions, this investment also provides an inflation hedge because rents historically rise in response to increases in the cost of living. Rent increases should also be reflected in an increased value of the real estate at the time it's sold.

The growth equity mutual fund carries the potential of long-term capital growth with average stock market risk. The Manalapans recognize that part or all the income realized on the fund's capital gain and dividend distributions will be taxed to Peter at the parents' higher tax bracket while he is under age 14. The international equity mutual fund enables the Manalapans to participate in the growth potential of the world economy. They understand and are willing to accept currency risk and market risk in return for the prospect of a premium return over the long term.

If the Manalapans average 8% a year after taxes on their college fund, they will have $193,000 on hand for Peter in 1997, which will probably be enough to finance his way through MIT, Rensselaer, or any other of the fifty most expensive four-year colleges in the U.S.

LATE STARTERS

College-Fund Investment Selection Guide (Child's age: 13–15)

Least risk

Savings accounts
U.S. savings bonds
Money-market funds
Certificates of deposit
Treasury bills
Short- to intermediate-term U.S. government bonds, including zero bonds, if held to maturity
CollegeSure CD

Little risk

Short- to intermediate-term investment-grade corporate bonds (rated Baa or higher) and unit investment trusts of these bonds held to maturity
Short- to intermediate-term investment-grade or insured municipal bonds and unit investment trusts of these bonds held to maturity

Moderate risk
Balanced, growth-income, and growth mutual funds
Common stocks of major companies with seasoned earnings and dividend performance records

Higher risk
Government securities mutual funds
Investment-grade corporate-bond funds
Municipal-bond mutual funds
Convertible bonds and preferred stock
Aggressive-growth mutual funds
Real Estate Investment Trusts

Strategy

Whether you are just starting to build a college fund at this point or have already established a fund, you must now be mindful of interest-rate risk, market risk, and illiquidity, because you have only three to five years until you start tapping the fund to pay expenses. That's why investment options for your college fund at this point are narrower than for Early Planners and certain investments are ranked as more inherently risky for you.

Illiquid investments such as real-estate limited partnerships with projected liquidation dates of eight to twelve years are no longer appropriate investments for your new savings. You also do not want to be in the position of having to liquidate a fixed-income security before it matures to meet college expenses if interest rates have gone up since you purchased it because the value of your bond may then be depressed. Long-term fixed-income securities such as U.S. government bonds, corporate bonds, and municipal bonds are particularly vulnerable to this interest-rate risk. For the same reason, you don't want your college fund to be overly exposed to market risk in common stocks or equity mutual funds.

As you consider risks, you must take into account your cash flow and investments other than your college fund. If your college fund were to fall in value because of market conditions, could you make up a shortfall from cash flow or income from those other investments?

By this point, you should be phasing out long-term fixed income investments, such as U.S. government bonds and municipal bonds with maturities *beyond* the years when you're scheduled to be meeting college bills, and mutual funds invested in long-term government securities, corporate bonds, and municipal bonds. Replace them with investments concentrated in short- to intermediate-term fixed-income securities and with unit investment trusts of bonds that mature to match the years when you'll be meeting college expenses.

You do not necessarily have to eliminate common stocks and equity mutual funds from your college fund by this time. If your child is only 13 years old, for instance, you still have eight to nine years until you pay the last college tuition bill. That is likely to be enough time to take you through two market cycles, giving you an opportunity to sell your shares during an up-cycle. Your personal financial situation, ability and desire to assume risk, and the rate of return you want to achieve on your college fund all go into making this decision.

College-Fund Savings Plan: Examples for Late Starters with Older Children

Elizabeth and Ted Tsai have two children: Naline, age 13, and Lionel, age 15. Their combined gross income is $55,000 a year and they are in the 28% tax bracket.

The Tsais have already saved $70,000, which they're ready to commit to meeting their children's college expenses. They estimate that they can continue to save $7,500 a year for this purpose.

With Lionel starting college in less than three years, the Tsais do not want to take any risk of losing capital in their college fund and have invested it mostly in municipal bonds which mature in eight to ten years.

They decide to sell these municipal bonds and invest in:

Six-month CD (When the CD matures in 1990, the Tsais intend to purchase Series EE savings bonds with the proceeds.)	$15,000
Staggered portfolio of short-term and intermediate-term insured municipal bonds maturing from 1992 through 1996	$50,000

After a great deal of thought, the Tsais settled on a very conservative college fund with tax advantages.

Based on their estimated adjusted gross income, they will probably be able to take full advantage of the tax exemption for interest earned on the Series EE savings bonds they use to pay college tuition. Since they will be able to hold the EE bonds five years, they can count on receiving at least the minimum interest-rate guarantee on the bonds.

For the Tsais, it was a close call between investing in the insured municipals or in U.S. Treasury bonds maturing from 1992 to 1996. At the time they were making their decision, they could have invested in Treasuries that yielded about 9.5% to maturity. They live in a high-income-tax state and so benefit from the fact that interest income on Treasuries is not subject to state or local taxes. The yield to maturity on insured municipal bonds at the time was about 7.5%, so their after-tax yield on Treasuries and municipals was particularly close.

Finally, the Tsais settled on the municipals because they decided there was some risk that federal income-tax rates would go up while they held the securities in their college fund. The interest on the municipal bonds is exempt from federal income taxes and the maturity schedule of the bonds matches the years of college education.

The Tsais are likely to be able to achieve an after-tax return of 8% on their college fund, which will increase its value to $129,000 by 1993. And they will add at least another $15,000 by the time Naline starts college in 1995. If they keep up their savings level, they will be able to contribute another $30,000 during the four years she is in college. That $174,000 total should cover tuition for both children at excellent schools.

Freda and Karl Reaser have a 14-year-old daughter, Holly. Their combined income is $100,000 a year, putting them in the 33% marginal federal tax bracket. They have not segregated their savings into a college fund but do have a personal investment portfolio with a current value of $75,000.

The Reasers are now anxious about meeting anticipated college costs and have worked out a budget to save $13,200 a year, a level of savings they believe they can sustain through 1996, when Holly would be expected to complete college. Their projected annual cash flow is good and they are willing to take moderate risk with their college-fund investments.

The Reasers own some common stock which they purchased for $9,000 a few years ago and it now has a value of $20,000. They would like to sell these shares in order to diversify the college-fund investments, but have been holding back because they are concerned about the income-tax consequences of a sale.

The Reasers decide to establish a Uniform Transfers to Minors Act (UTMA) custodial account for Holly at a brokerage firm and make a gift of the appreciated stock to the account. The custodian of the UTMA account, a family friend, will sell the shares. The gain will then be taxed to Holly at her 15% tax bracket instead of the Reasers' 33% bracket. This conserves almost $2,000 for their daughter's college fund.

The Reasers recommend that the custodian invest the $18,300 after-tax sale proceeds in:

Zero-coupon U.S. Treasury bond (maturing at $13,000 in 1993)	$10,000
Growth mutual fund	$8,300

The interest accumulated on the zero-coupon Treasury bond will be taxed each year at Holly's 15% tax bracket. The bond also assures Holly of $13,000 in 1993, when she starts her freshman year.

The Reasers appreciate the market risk associated with a growth mutual fund. They select a fund that has historically underperformed the market in up years but *outperformed the market in down years.* With some of the first year's tuition covered by the zero-coupon Treasury bond, they feel comfortable adding some growth potential to the college fund in the four years ahead of them before they start paying college expenses. They intend to monitor the fund's performance and could sell fund shares before four years, after reassessing their financial position, the performance of both the stock market and their fund, and their education cost requirements.

The Reasers' plan is to make an annual gift of $13,200 to the UTMA account, which will be invested primarily in low-risk, income-producing securities, to take advantage of Holly's 15% tax bracket.

If Holly's college fund earns 8% after tax, there will be approximately $65,000 available in three years by the time she's ready for college. That, plus the sums the Reasers continue to contribute while Holly is in college will be enough to pay tuition at a number of excellent schools, including Santa Clara in California, Colorado College, Ohio Wesleyan, or Macalester and St. Olaf in Minnesota.

LAST-MINUTE SAVERS

College-Fund Investment Selection Guide (Child's age: 16–18)

Least risk

Savings accounts
Money-market funds
Certificates of deposit
Treasury bills
U.S. savings bonds
Short- to intermediate-term U.S. government bonds, including zero bonds, if held to maturity
CollegeSure CD

Little risk

Short- to intermediate-term investment-grade corporate bonds (rated Baa or higher) and unit investment trusts of these bonds held to maturity
Short- to intermediate-term investment-grade or insured municipal bonds and unit investment trusts held to maturity

Moderate risk

Balanced mutual funds

Higher risk

Government securities mutual funds
Investment-grade corporate-bond mutual funds
Municipal-bond mutual funds
Growth-income and growth mutual funds

Strategy

With your child so close to college, your college fund should be concentrated in investments that minimize or eliminate market and/or interest-rate risk.

You can accomplish that by concentrating the holdings in your college fund in short-term fixed-income investments and cash investments, such as CDs, Treasury bills, and money-market funds. Maturities on all fixed-income securities, such as bonds and unit investment trusts of bonds, should approximate the time when you will need the cash to meet college expenses.

You cannot afford to assume any market risk if a sharp decline in the stock market during the next six years would leave you without enough financial resources to see your child through college. If that is your situation, phase out stocks and equity mutual funds, particularly if your child is 18 or older.

THE COLLEGE YEARS

While your child is attending college, your college fund has maximum need for both capital preservation and liquidity. You can achieve that by maintaining your holdings in:

Savings accounts
Money-market funds
Certificates of deposit
Treasury bills
Short- to intermediate-term U.S. government bonds, including zero bonds, scheduled to mature as needed to meet college expenses
Short- to intermediate-term investment-grade corporate bonds (rated Baa or higher) and unit investment trusts of those bonds scheduled to mature as needed to meet college expenses
Short- to intermediate-term investment-grade or insured municipal bonds and unit investment trusts scheduled to mature as needed to meet college expenses

III. UNDERSTANDING YOUR CHOICES

Once you've identified the most appropriate investments for your college fund in Part Two, use this section for the basic information you need to ask the right questions and make the wisest choices as an intelligent consumer.

6

The Trade-offs in Building Your College Fund

Just as there is no right or wrong way to spend money, so, too, there is no right or wrong way to distribute your savings among different investments. Of course, some money trade-offs are not always conscious or obvious: a night on the town or a new silk blouse; upgrade the stereo system or buy a small Oriental rug. Investment decisions, on the other hand, are much more deliberate and anxiety provoking. Choices seem more complex. The sums of money involved are usually large relative to, say, the checks you write every month to pay bills. And many people suffer from a lurking fear that the wrong investment choice can simply vaporize value—leaving you with less than if you spent the money instead on a stereo system or silk blouse.

It doesn't take any more skill or knowledge, however, to be an intelligent investor and preserve the growing value of your savings than it takes to be an intelligent consumer.

As your college fund grows, the chief trade-off you'll have to make again and again is between risk and return. In an environment of relatively low inflation, an investment that you expect to return 12% a year almost inevitably will be more risky than one that returns 8%. Since college tuitions are consistently being pushed up at a rate higher than the general inflation rate, it's tempting to think you have to concentrate on high-return investments. That would be a mistake. College-fund investing should be conservative, say PaineWebber's experts. If your priority is to have something substantial set aside so that your child can consider a wider choice of top-quality colleges when the time comes, focus on two other factors before you worry about how much your investments will earn:

- Time. Nothing you can do is more powerful than saving consistently over the longest period of time.
- Your savings rate. Take a hard look at what your family's priorities really are.

If you anticipate falling short of what you would like to have for your child, don't try to make up the difference by taking high risks with your savings. That's gambling, not investing. Student and family educational loans, financial aid, and a rigorous search for high-quality schools with lower tuitions that meet your child's particular needs are far better alternatives.

Even limiting your selections to fairly conservative investments, you'll find ample variety in the chapters that follow.

Each of the remaining chapters in Part Three is devoted to a specific type of investment. Chapter Seven, "Cash: The Right Ways to Handle It," discusses what to do with your money as you're building it up for a special investment, say a $1,000 zero Treasury bond. Chapters Eight and Nine, "Funds and Unit Investment Trusts" and "Zero Bonds," give you essential information on how to evaluate and wisely invest in stocks and bonds "packaged" in these special forms. The chapters that follow these two start with the lowest-risk investments and continue through to higher-risk investments still appropriate for your college fund.

To simplify the differences between investment alternatives and to help you compare one to another, we've discussed them under four broad categories whenever possible: What They Are, What You Must Know Before Making a Choice, and How to Buy Wisely. You will see these categories repeated throughout each investment choice in Part Three. You also will find information on the risks and appropriateness of each investment for a college fund, selection guidelines developed with the help of PaineWebber experts, information on keeping track of investments, and other special considerations specific to each choice.

7

Cash: The Right Ways to Handle It

Before you start to consider investments for your college fund, make sure you have control of the cash you'll quickly build up once you're an aggressive saver. You should no longer think of cash as the bills in your wallet, the balance in your checking account, and the money earning the absolute minimum in a savings account. Instead, treat cash as they do in the hard-edged world of professional investing—as cash-equivalents: liquid investments that earn twenty-four hours a day, seven days a week, and can be easily tapped. As an individual investor, you don't have access to as wide a sweep of choices as the professionals have. But you can't afford to be slapdash, either, because you'll soon be dealing with substantial sums. You'll have a personal liquidity fund for emergencies—at least 10% of your assets (aside from your home or condo) or six months of expenses. You'll have the cash you accumulate month by month to deploy in longer-term investments. You may have interest and dividend earnings from the investments in your college fund that aren't automatically reinvested. And, finally, when you're close to putting the college fund to use, you'll want most of it to be highly liquid—to write checks for tuition, room and board, books, and transportation expenses.

Review the following options for keeping your cash. You're sure to find a combination that's as convenient as stashing it all in a checking account and a lot more profitable, too.

MONEY-MARKET ACCOUNTS AND FUNDS

The bank you use for your checking account probably also offers a money-market account. These accounts are covered by the bank's deposit insurance and are generally designed to offer bank customers a higher yield than a "passbook" savings account and easier access to their money than bank certificates of deposit (CDs) allow. The interest rate offered on bank money-market accounts depends on the bank's eagerness to attract deposits and rates often change from week to week.

A money-market fund, on the other hand, is a mutual fund (we'll discuss mutual funds in more detail in Chapter Eight) that buys short-term debt securities, such as Treasury bills and commercial paper (the short-term debt issued by companies). Money-market funds are *not* covered by federal insurance but have an excellent record of safety. Since they buy securities that mature in a few days or months, they face minimal risk that they will have to sell any of them for less than face value.

The yields available on money-market funds are driven by market rates of interest on the short-term paper they purchase. The money-market fund's yield is quoted as an annual percentage rate—say 7.2%—but changes as short-term interest rates change. So, when interest rates move up sharply, yields on money-market funds may move up more quickly than the rates offered by bank money-market accounts. Money-market fund rates may fall more quickly, too, when interest rates start to slide.

The difference between what you can earn on a bank money-market account and a money-market fund is heavily dependent on the way banks choose to compete with money-market funds for deposits. Ordinarily, the insurance on the bank money-market accounts could be expected to be worth about half a percentage point—that is, money-market *funds* would have to pay at least that much *more* to attract cash. The difference can grow to three percentage points, however. In the spring of 1989, for instance, many bank money-market accounts were paying an average of about 6.5% while money-market mutual funds were paying about 9.5%. Interest rates were going up, which was being reflected in higher money-market fund yields. But many bankers weren't following the rates up, they said, because they didn't want to compete for "hot" money that simply moved in and out as rates changed. Instead, many banks raised their rates aggressively on CDs.

If some of your college fund is invested in a family of mutual funds—say, a growth-stock fund or a bond fund (more about this in Chapter Eight), you probably can easily use the family's money-market fund, too. Or you may use an asset-management account with your broker that "sweeps" interest and dividend payments on your investments into a particular money-market fund. If your tax bracket warrants, select the fund family's tax-free money-market fund.

Most money-market funds offer check-writing privileges and a telephone-switching service that enables you to phone in to withdraw money or move it to your bank or to another fund. At the time you open your fund account, be sure to ask for and sign all the forms necessary to take advantage of these services. You want to be able to put your hands on this cash or move it around as quickly as possible when necessary.

TREASURY BILLS

If you have at least $10,000 to keep liquid, you can buy a Treasury bill that matures in 90 days, 180 days, or one year. The interest earned on T-bills, as they are called, is exempt from state and local taxes. This exemption can raise the effective yield half a point or so above the stated yield for someone in a high-tax state.

To protect your principal, T-bills are absolutely the safest investments you can make. So, when T-bills pay more than you can get in a money-market account or bank CD, you should be alert to the advantage of shifting funds you want to keep liquid into them. Be sure, of course, that the T-bills mature no later than the time you need the cash to meet college bills.

You can buy T-bills from your broker (for a fee of about $25 to $60 per $10,000 bill). This may be convenient for you if you have most of your college fund in a brokerage account, because the T-bill investments will also be reported on your statement, making it easy to keep track of your progress.

You can also buy T-bills directly from your nearest Federal Reserve Bank, either in person or by mail without paying a fee. (A list of all Federal Reserve Banks and their addresses and phone numbers is in the Appendix.) It is now very simple to set up an account with the

U.S. Treasury that enables you to buy new issues of T-bills, and either reinvest automatically or have the proceeds flow directly to your bank when the bills mature. (See Chapter Ten for details.) This Treasury Direct Account is a useful way to maintain some portion of your college fund in safe, short-term securities. It then can become a vehicle for holding liquid assets safely when your fund is near completion and you want an easy way to earn income up until you transfer funds into your checking account—and write a tuition check.

The Treasury auctions three- and six-month T-bills every business Monday and twelve-month bills every fourth Thursday. You can find the latest rate established in the Monday auction on Tuesday in the financial pages of your local newspaper. These rates are also listed in the "Money Rates" feature in every issue of *The Wall Street Journal.* When you fill in your application for a Treasury bill (see Chapter Ten for details), check that it is a "noncompetitive" bid, which means you'll get the average auction rate. (Competitive bidders are the giant securities firms that buy most of the bill offerings.)

You'll actually be earning more, on an annual basis, on your T-bill than the listed auction rate. That's because bills are sold on what's called an "original issue discount basis." You send in a certified check or bank teller check for $10,000. The weekly auction establishes the discount—say, $208 for a 8.21% yield on a 13-week bill, which is what the Tuesday papers report. The Treasury sends the $208 to your bank account within three working days of the date the bills are issued, so you've actually invested $9,792. Then, in 26 weeks, when the bill matures, you receive $10,000 back. (The whole transaction is a book entry only; you never receive an actual bill certificate.)

The true annual yield in this example is 8.5% and it's calculated by using the following formula, which you can apply yourself when computing what you're actually earning on a T-bill investment for your college fund:

$$\frac{10{,}000 - \text{price } (9{,}792) = 208}{\text{price } (9{,}792)} \times \frac{365}{\text{days to mature } (91)} = .0852\ (8.5\%)$$

On a calculator that's:

$$\frac{208 \times 365}{9{,}792 \times 91} = \frac{75{,}920}{891{,}072} = 75{,}920 \div 891{,}072 = .0852\ (8.5\%)$$

CERTIFICATES OF DEPOSIT

A CD is a financial instrument showing that you have placed a *specific* sum of money on deposit for a *specific* period of time at a *specific* rate of interest. Your return on a CD is generally higher on a pre-tax basis than what's available on U.S. Treasury securities although it may be lower on an after-tax basis, depending on your individual tax bracket. CDs, however, are not as liquid as a money-market account or money-market fund since the shortest term usually offered is three months.

If you withdraw your money from a CD before it matures, most banks charge an interest penalty. But the penalty is not required by law and in many areas of the country banks now offer CDs from which you can withdraw at set intervals. Balancing off this flexibility feature, however, the initial rate on these CDs is often a bit lower than what is available on CDs that lock in your cash with the penalty clause.

Widen your horizons when shopping for CDs these days. You may actually find your best CD rate via your securities broker—often in an out-of-state bank but sometimes even on a bank in your own city. Many banks offer brokers a fee to bring in CD deposits and make themselves attractive to brokerage customers by offering rates higher than those available to people walking in off the street to open CD accounts. For many brokers, this is a "loss leader" business, offered as a service to customers. No commissions are charged. The same $100,000 insurance limits provided by the Federal Deposit Insurance Corporation (for banks) and Federal Savings and Loan Insurance Corporation (for savings and loans) apply. But if you are concerned about troubled banks and savings-and-loans, make sure your broker tells you what he knows about the financial health of the savings institution before you invest in its CDs.

Many securities dealers also maintain a secondary market in CDs, which means they may be able to sell your CD for you before it matures, if necessary. Of course, if you want to sell because rates are going up, buyers will be scarce; you'll probably only be able to sell by taking a loss on the value of your CD. That loss could be greater than the penalty a bank would levy for cashing in a CD before maturity.

Don't be afraid to negotiate with a local bank if you're ready to invest a substantial sum in a CD, which could be the case when you are near the end of building your college fund. You can just about always negotiate a higher CD rate from a bank or savings-and-loan for a "jumbo CD"—$100,000 or more. And many banks are now offering higher rates for "mini jumbos" as small as $25,000. If you wind up investing over the $100,000 deposit insurance limit in a bank, ask the advice of a bank officer on breaking up the deposit into separate accounts that will be fully covered.

Look at the financial pages of your local newspaper on Thursday or Friday, when they usually carry information on rates available in banks and savings-and-loans in the area. You'll probably also spot ads from out-of-state banks looking for deposits and generally offering rates above those offered by your local banks.

In the recent past, savings-and-loans and savings banks (called thrifts) in financially troubled areas of the country have offered rates two percentage points or more above the national average to lure in CD deposits. Because serious problems have developed with many savings-and-loan companies, federal banking regulators now send in examiners quickly when they suspect that a troubled bank is advertising for deposits with excessively high rates.

Many investors have been willing to take the risk for the higher yield. Beware. Not all banks and savings-and-loans are federally insured. And even if they are deposit insurance doesn't cover other risks:

- Investors who have more than $100,000 in a failed institution, even if it is in several different accounts *under the same name,* will not be insured for more than $100,000. However, deposits maintained in different rights and capacities—IRAs and individual accounts, for example—*are* each separately insured to $100,000. Make sure you get expert advice from a bank officer on how to set up CD accounts that will be fully insured if you decide to put more than $100,000 in a single institution.
- Compared to local depositors, out-of-state depositors are at a disadvantage when an insolvent bank is closed or has its deposits transferred. Bank regulators usually send out letters informing depositors that they will pay off up to $100,000 per account limit within 48 days of the closing. Local depositors usually can get to the bank the next day to withdraw their CDs without penalty—but not out-of-staters.
- If the insured deposits in a troubled bank or savings-and-loan are transferred to another bank, it may honor the old CD rates for only thirty days.

- It might cost up to $100 (for notary fees, express mail, wire-transfer fees, and lost interest) to get your money out of a failed bank.
- Your matured CD may be frozen for several weeks at a failed bank or savings-and-loan, earning a low passbook-savings account rate of interest until the cash is released to you. Both the FDIC and FSLIC are working out arrangements to speed up these payments, however, and some depositors have been able to withdraw their cash within 48 hours of the shutdown of a failed bank or savings-and-loan.

As the yield differences continue to narrow between healthy and unhealthy banks, college-fund investors probably ought to avoid the risky ones altogether. You can do your own research before you make a CD deposit in a thrift by asking for its latest quarterly financial report, available (on written request only) from the Federal Home Loan Bank Board, 1700 G Street NW, Washington, DC 20552. Key ratio: A minimum capital-to-asset ratio of 3%. A private company compiles the data on thrifts and publishes a quarterly "Troubled Thrift List" and "Safest Thrift List." Each list is available for $10 from Bauer Communications, P.O. Drawer 145510, Coral Gables, FL 33114.

HANDLING YOUR CASH SAFELY AND WISELY

Give convenience and easy accessibility a great deal of consideration in selecting the right place to put your cash, since money-market funds, money-market accounts, T-bills, and CDs all rank high for safety. Differences in yield among the four shift and often are not very significant. When short-term interest rates rise, the rates on all four will go up (though not always in tandem), and they'll drift down together, too, when rates drop.

To discipline your savings during the early days of building up the college fund, you might want to arrange for an automatic monthly or twice-monthly transfer of funds from your checking account into a money-market fund. Then, you can write checks from the fund to make any other investments in your plan. An asset-management account at a brokerage firm will also tie together your holdings. These techniques will simplify your record-keeping, too, since you'll see exactly what you saved and where it went.

Probably the least effective way to manage your cash is to spend a lot of time searching around for the highest rates on CDs and putting your cash into a variety of banks and savings-and-loans at different maturities, depending on which banks have special promotions for deposits. You'll find it increasingly hard to keep track of what's where, what's about to mature, and what the rate will be if you reinvest a maturing CD at the same bank. Like most busy people in that situation, you'll probably forget to instruct a bank now and then about what to do. Then, chances are good that you'll wind up with your cash reinvested at an unattractive rate for an inconvenient term and face a penalty if you try to get your hands on your money. Buying your CDs through your broker, who sends you a monthly report on your account, eases this monitoring and record-keeping task.

Toward the end of your college-fund building, however, when you have most of your assets in liquid investments, look for especially attractive rates on CDs that mature just when you know you will have to write a substantial tuition check. Otherwise, be sure to have the money on tap in a money-market account, earning something right up to the time the college cashes your check.

A SPECIAL CD FOR COLLEGE SAVING

The CollegeSure® CD, originated by the College Savings Bank in Princeton, New Jersey, is a special CD that earns interest at a rate directly linked to increases in the cost of a college education. Obviously, this unique product is less like a conventional CD in which you simply park your cash. It's more a long-term way of saving for college. It offers you a way to ensure that your savings grow at a rate sufficient to reach the sum needed for college.

The rate you receive on your CollegeSure CD is not set by market rates of interest but is linked to the change in the Independent College 500 Index™, calculated and published annually by the College Board. This Index measures the rate of change for tuition, fees, room and board incurred by full-time freshmen at five hundred private four-year colleges and universities. (About 75% of the nation's undergraduates attend these five hundred schools.)

Each July 31, the interest at a rate determined by the Index is credited to your CollegeSure CD Account. The interest you receive will average one point below the Index increase if you have invested in a CollegeSure CD of $10,000 or more, or one and a half points below if your original CD investment was the minimum $1,000.

The goal is to have the money you invest in a CollegeSure CD increase in value in close relation to the overall increase in costs at private colleges. The bank also guarantees a minimum return of 4% a year, should the rate of college inflation suddenly decline to below that rate (which isn't too likely).

CollegeSure CDs are FDIC-insured and are top-rated (AAA-L) by Standard & Poor's. Maturities are available for one to twenty-five years. If you change your mind about sticking with the CollegeSure CD, you can withdraw interest without penalty. But you *will* be charged a penalty for withdrawing principal before maturity—10% for withdrawing during the first to third year, 1% for withdrawing during the year of maturity but prior to July 31, and 5% for withdrawing any other year.

There could be times when the CollegeSure CD rate is greater than market rates for CDs. And it could also be lower than those rates at times. What you get in return, however, is peace of mind of a different sort: your investment continues to grow in direct relation to college-cost inflation.

The CollegeSure CD is not primarily a cash-equivalent investment such as the conventional CDs, T-bills, and money-market investments covered earlier in this chapter. It could function more as a foundation for a conservatively managed college fund, just as zero-coupon bonds might do. Unlike zeros, however, the CollegeSure CD will keep pace with costs at a representative group of colleges, no matter how high those costs rise.

The CollegeSure CD can be purchased directly from the College Savings Bank in Princeton, New Jersey, or through PaineWebber. There is no difference in cost between the two.

Appropriateness guide

The minimum investment to open a CollegeSure Account is $1,000 and you then can purchase additional CollegeSure CDs for as little as $250 at any time, which allows you to build your college fund over time.

CollegeSure CDs are available in a wide range of maturities so they can be used at any stage in building a college fund, though *Early Planners* and *Late Starters* will find them most appropriate.

8

Funds and Unit Investment Trusts: Packages for Your College-Fund Investments

You'll regularly have to make choices, as your college-fund assets build up, between investing directly in a security, such as a bond or share of stock, or buying them bundled into a package, either as a mutual fund, closed-end fund, or a unit investment trust (UIT). Treasury bonds and bills, bank certificates of deposit, company stocks and bonds, municipal bonds, and many other types of securities and mixtures of securities are now all available in funds or UITs.

You may have heard that funds and UITs are for so-called passive investors and direct bond and stock purchases for active investors. That's not true. There's nothing more passive about selecting the right fund or UIT than there is about picking a particular stock or bond. Furthermore, many of the best stock and bond selections you make for your college fund may well be buy-and-hold decisions. This differs little from sticking with a fund that fits the way you've decided to accumulate your money.

Far more important in making a decision between directly owning a security or buying a fund is your tolerance for risk. One long-proven way to reduce risk is by diversifying investments—the investment equivalent of the familiar advice not to "put all your eggs in one basket." You can diversify by holding a variety of investments (shares in companies in a number of different industries, plus Treasuries and municipals, etc.). And you can diversify to reduce your risk in a certain type of security (by investing in municipal bonds issued by a variety of different public entities, for instance).

The goal is the same: If one issue goes sour or a particular kind of security comes under market pressure, the impact on your investment holdings will be limited. Funds and UITs offer a level of diversification hard for you to match when buying individual securities. Some kinds of securities you probably ought to consider investing in *only* via a fund or UIT such as high-yield (junk) bonds. As an individual investor, you could be taking too high a risk or losing liquidity by owning just a few individual high-yield corporate or municipal bonds.

As your college fund grows, you're likely to find yourself with a mix of investments, some in funds and UITs and some in directly owned securities. That's usually a sound approach for most people. You must know what to look for, though, when you make the choice.

In this section, you'll find what mutual funds, closed-end funds, and UITs have to offer and general guidelines on selecting the ones that best match up with what you need at particular stages of building your college fund. (The types of funds or UITs that you might consider, depending on your child's age and your tolerance for risk, are listed in the Investment Guides in Part Two of this book.) In this section of the book, you'll find specific information on funds and UITs for Treasuries, municipal bonds, and company bonds and stocks in each of the chapters dealing with those securities.

MUTUAL FUNDS

When you invest in a mutual fund, you pool your savings with those of many other investors, put the money under professional management, and benefit from diversification, which spreads your risk over a wider group of securities than you could invest in yourself.

What Mutual Funds Are

You can virtually always purchase and redeem shares in a mutual fund, which is why they are also called open-end funds. The initial minimum investment is generally low, usually between $250 and $1,000 to open a fund account. Subsequent purchases of fund shares can usually be made for even less. All mutual funds allow you to automatically reinvest your dividends and capital gains into additional shares of the fund. Occasionally, however, managers of particularly successful funds decide that money is flowing in too fast to be invested properly, and the fund will be temporarily closed to new investors.

Each mutual fund strives for certain investment objectives and goals: preservation of capital, income, or growth of capital. Preservation of capital is a risk measure. A fund that manages to preserve capital will generally be less volatile than the average fund. Income and growth of capital are measures of return. An income-oriented fund is geared to produce current income with growth as a secondary objective. A growth-oriented fund strives to produce capital gains, foregoing current income and risking volatility when necessary. Every fund must describe the type of securities in which it intends to invest, together with its investment objectives and goals, in the prospectus sent to you to review before you place an order. A growth fund prospectus, for instance, might state:

> The Fund's investment objective is capital appreciation. At least 65% of the Fund's assets normally will be invested in stocks of large, established U.S. companies. . . .

By contrast, an income fund prospectus could state:

> The Fund's primary objective is to achieve a high level of current income consistent with prudent investment risk by investing primarily in debt securities. Capital appreciation is a secondary objective. . . .

And a global fund prospectus could state:

> The Fund will invest primarily in common stocks of issuers based in the United States, Europe, Japan and the Pacific Basin.

An effective fund manager strives to minimize the risks and enhance the rewards available from the type of securities he trades by good market timing and careful selection. Nevertheless, the basic nature of each type of fund remains consistent at all times.

Descriptions of the sixteen basic types of mutual funds are listed in the table on page 93. The check (✓) marks next to each fund on the list indicate the relative importance of preservation of capital, income, and growth of capital to each of these funds. Those close to the top of the list make preservation of capital a major investment goal and so, in general, are the least risky. The four types of funds at the bottom of the list are, in the opinion of PaineWebber experts, generally less suitable for college funds, as are funds that invest in particular industries, such as energy or high-technology (so-called sector funds), because they are fairly volatile in price.

Depending on your tolerance for risk and the number of years you have before liquidating your college fund to pay tuition, you could be invested in three or four of these funds at a time. The menu seems large, but use the Investment Guides in Part Two to focus on the most suitable funds for your particular situation.

THE BASIC FUND TYPES: WHAT THEY INVEST IN AND WHAT THEIR GOALS ARE

0 = NOT A MAJOR INVESTMENT GOAL
✓ = A MAJOR INVESTMENT GOAL
✓✓ = A VERY IMPORTANT INVESTMENT GOAL

FUND	PRESERVATION OF CAPITAL	INCOME	GROWTH	FUND DESCRIPTION
U.S. GOVERNMENT	✓✓	✓	0	Invests in a variety of government securities.
GNMA (GINNIE MAE)	✓✓	✓	0	Invests most of the portfolio at all times in Government National Mortgage Association mortgage-backed securities.
GROWTH AND INCOME	0	✓	✓	Invests mainly in the common stock of companies with a solid record of paying dividends and an expectation of higher share value.
MUNICIPAL BOND	✓	✓✓	0	Invests in municipal bonds. In most cases income earned on these bonds is exempt from federal income tax, but may be taxed under state and local laws or may be subject to AMT.
STATE MUNICIPAL BOND	✓	✓✓	0	Invests in municipal bonds of one state. Income earned on these bonds is exempt from federal and state income tax but may be subject to AMT.

FUND	PRESERVATION OF CAPITAL	INCOME	GROWTH	FUND DESCRIPTION
INVESTMENT-GRADE CORPORATE BONDS	✓	✓✓	0	Invests two-thirds or more of the portfolio at all times in higher-rated (BBB or better by Moody's and Baa by Standard & Poor's—or better) corporate bonds.
INCOME	✓	✓✓	0	Seeks high current income by investing in a mix of corporate and government bonds.
EQUITY-INCOME	✓	✓✓	0	Seeks relatively high current income by investing primarily in equities of companies with good dividend-paying records.
GROWTH	0	0	✓✓	Invests in stock of companies with potential for long-term capital appreciation.
GLOBAL GROWTH	0	0	✓✓	Invests in stocks of companies traded worldwide, including securities of U.S. companies.
WORLD INCOME	✓	✓✓	0	Invests primarily in U.S.-dollar and non-U.S.-dollar debt instruments.
INTERNATIONAL	0	0	✓✓	Invests the portfolio at all times in equity securities of companies located outside the U.S.
AGGRESSIVE GROWTH	0	0	✓✓	Seeks maximum capital gains by investing in equities of undervalued companies. Some funds may employ investment strategies such as option writing or short-term trading.
HIGH-YIELD BOND	0	✓✓	0	Invests two-thirds or more of its portfolio at all times in lower-rated corporate bonds (Baa or lower by Moody's and BBB or lower by Standard & Poor's).
PRECIOUS METALS	0	0	✓✓	Invests two-thirds or more of the portfolio at all times in securities associated with gold, silver or other precious metals.
OPTION-INCOME	0	✓✓	0	Seeks high current return by investing in dividend-paying equities on which call options are written.

What You Must Know Before Making a Choice

It's easy to find out what mutual funds are worth. The key term is "net asset value." At the end of every trading day on the exchange, each fund calculates its net asset value per share by dividing the market value of all the securities in the fund's portfolio (less any liabilities such as accounts payable or accrued expenses) by the number of fund shares outstanding.

You can look up the net asset value of the fund shares you own in the financial pages of your daily newspaper or in *The Wall Street Journal.* The value of your own investment in the fund is the net asset value times the number of shares you own. For example, if the net asset value listed for your fund's shares is $10.50 and you own 500 shares, your holdings are worth $5,250 (500 × $10.50).

Funds generate income for their fund shareholders from the dividends and interest paid by the stocks and bonds in the funds' portfolios and also by trading those securities for capital gains.

Monitoring *total return* is the best way to keep track of the progress of your fund investment. Total return is simple common sense. For example, if you hold a fund share for a year and receive a $1 dividend but the net asset value of the fund declines from $10 to $9 per share, your assets haven't grown. You've made nothing, so your total return is 0%. If, on the other hand, the net asset value of your fund's shares went up to $11 (adding 10% in value) and you received that $1 dividend per share (another 10%), your total return would be 20%. A mutual fund calculates its total return over time by assuming that all dividends and capital gains are reinvested and compounded.

Look at total return when you're comparing the performance of various funds prior to selecting one in which to invest. The prospectus you receive from your broker or from a fund when you ask for information will report the fund's one-year, five-year, and ten-year total return (or the record for as long as the fund has existed, if that is less than five or ten years).

With that information, you'll know how well the fund itself did but not how its performance compares to funds invested in similar securities, or how well the fund did compared to the market itself. Your broker or the fund itself should be able to supply data comparing the fund's performance against market indicators, such as the Standard & Poor's 500 Index for stocks, or against various bond indices. Once you are interested in fund investments, pick up the issues of *Money, Forbes, Business Week,* or *Barron's* that rank the performance of hundreds of funds every three months. You'll also find some funds ranked every day in *The Wall Street Journal*'s "Mutual Fund Monitor."

Check, too, how the fund fared when the market declined. The quarterly mutual-fund performance tables prepared by financial publications usually use some technique to assess this performance and then rank the fund by "risk." The funds that do better than their peers in down-markets are considered less risky and usually follow what are called "defensive" investing strategies. Generally, this means they are *not* the top performers during strong bull markets.

How to Buy Mutual Funds Wisely

If you are a Late Starter on your college plan, you might prefer the less volatile funds. An Early Planner, however, might focus more on a fund's long-term total return and less on its defensive character.

Mutual funds are generally long-term investments. Instant appreciation is a possibility but is more the exception than the rule.

Long-term fund investing provides the easiest way to practice a time-proven technique called dollar-cost averaging. This means investing a fixed amount of dollars in a fund at regular intervals rather than buying shares sporadically. If your check to the fund, for instance, is $500 a month, you will buy more shares when they are priced lower (say, 83.3 shares at $6 a share) than when they are priced higher (only 50 shares at $10 a share).

So long as the market is in a long-term upward trend (which it has been since the 1950s), study after study shows that by dollar-cost averaging you're much more likely to accumulate your shares at a lower average cost per share than by buying sporadically. Thus, you maximize your gains when you sell.

To reap the most benefits from this technique, you must invest over a complete market cycle (a period of time that includes both a down-market and an up-market), which typically means at least six years or so. If you dollar-cost average over ten years or more, it generally doesn't even matter whether you start to invest in a bear market or a bull market.

The table on page 97 illustrates how dollar-cost averaging works.

Above all, don't be swayed by a fund's most recent performance. This is key to intelligent selection. Securities markets run in cycles, with certain issues in favor or out of favor at various times. Because interest rates and other economic factors change, the investment strategy that worked best in the recent past may not work at all in the immediate future. Look, at least, at the fund's *five-year* record. The ten-year record is very significant, too, if the same managers are in charge of the fund. If they've moved on (occasionally they are lured away by competitors), the past performance is a less useful guide. (Your broker can get this information for you on funds he or she handles. If you're dealing directly with a fund, ask the fund representative.)

THE ADVANTAGE OF DOLLAR-COST AVERAGING

FUND SHARE PRICE	QUARTERLY INVESTMENT	NUMBER OF SHARES PURCHASED	CUMULATIVE AVERAGE COST PER SHARE
$10	$1,000	100	$10.00
9	1,000	111	9.48
8	1,000	125	8.93
7	1,000	143	8.35
6	1,000	167	7.74
5	1,000	200	7.09
6	1,000	167	6.91
7	1,000	143	6.92
8	1,000	125	7.03
9	1,000	111	7.18
10	1,000	100	7.37

You should exercise caution when buying equity-oriented funds at the end of the year, when most successful mutual funds make a big payout (called a "distribution") of capital gains and dividends. The net asset value of the shares usually drops when the dividends and capital gains flow out to shareholders. The shares go "ex dividend" (indicated by a small *x* next to the listed net asset value), which means that if you buy the shares at that price you won't get that latest distribution of income. It pays to wait to buy at the ex-dividend price if you are about to make a fund investment around that time, unless you are buying shares in a tax-free fund. The trap to avoid is buying a few days earlier, before the shares are available ex dividend. You will pay the higher price *and immediately incur taxable income for the year for the value of the distribution—which is really your own money coming back to you.*

Once you've decided on a particular type of fund and identified one with a satisfactory performance level, pay some attention to the relative costs of buying various funds. You'll pay a sales charge on a fund bought through a securities firm, to meet the expense of providing personal service to you in making a choice. Some sales charges are paid at the time you purchase fund shares (called a *front-load*), and they range downward from 8.5% of the total sum invested. Usually the larger the investment, the lower the rate of the sales charge. Ask your broker to explain where the "breakpoints" are (where the rate drops down to the next lowest level) to help you decide wisely how much to invest. Other funds put your entire investment to work for you at the start by avoiding an up-front charge, but they levy an exit (or redemption) fee that can range from 6% down to zero if you sell the fund within five to seven years of the day of purchase. After that, there's no exit fee. These funds are called *reverse-load* or *back-end-load* funds.

Reverse-load funds also usually take a distribution fee (called a 12b-1 fee) every year from the fund that can amount to 1% or more of the shareholder's assets.

No-load funds, which do not charge up-front, back-end, or distribution fees, are available directly from the funds themselves, which usually advertise with a toll-free number for information and applications.

All funds, of course, have to charge fees for management and administration. A fund that sends you a monthly check, for instance, rather than a simple account statement, is very likely to run at a higher cost. All of these costs, and other fees and commissions, are clearly reported in a fund's prospectus.

Remember to put all these costs into perspective, relating them to the fund's performance and to the service you need and expect to get.

With so much information about fund investment goals, performance, and costs available, don't lose sight of a simple strategy: *Pick a family of funds rather than a series of unrelated funds.* Many investment firms have developed their own fund families. These fund families include a wide variety of stock, bond, tax-free, growth, and money-market funds. Many fund companies also offer a wide range of funds. The advantage of staying within a family is that you can move from fund to fund in the group, or shift part of your assets to another fund, by paying a small fee ($5 or so). You can also often arrange to have the income from one fund flow into another fund.

Even though you will not be doing a lot of fund switching, these conveniences can be considerable for a long-term fund investor. Simpler record-keeping alone may make it worthwhile. So, if you find a fund family that has what you want and is generally above average in its performance and moderate in its costs, don't give up convenience for the apparent advantage of investing in a number of unrelated funds, each of which appears to offer some small benefit.

How to Keep Track of Your Mutual-Fund Investment

It's very important to maintain accurate mutual-fund records, because those fund shares eventually will be sold. You may also switch the types of funds you're in as your child gets closer to college age, or you may transfer ownership. Whether you shift to another fund in the family or sell shares outright, you often trigger a tax liability.

By keeping good records you can:

- Maintain a simple record of your funds' performance by jotting down dividends and capital gains reinvested each quarter or month and the net asset value at that time. While doing this, multiply the net asset value per share by the number of shares you own to see how your assets are building.
- Control the type and amount of gain or loss you report when you sell fund shares (or exchange them for another fund in the family, which is also regarded as a redemption).
- Avoid the all-too-common mistake of paying taxes twice on reinvested fund dividends.

Set up a folder for each fund and *keep every statement from the fund or brokerage firm* that shows the price at which you purchased shares, the date they were purchased, and whether the shares were purchased with reinvested dividends.

Armed with that information, you can instruct the fund to *sell the shares purchased at the highest price first,* so you realize the lowest capital gain. Photocopy the letter instructing the fund to make the sale or exchange the shares and staple it together with a photocopy of the confirmation statement showing when you purchased the shares and how much you paid for them. When you get the fund's transaction statement on the sale, chances are it will not specify which shares it sold. That's why it is so important to have your own record of your instructions to the fund; you'll need verification of specific transactions if you are audited by the IRS.

If you cannot identify your purchases by date and price, the IRS will generally insist that your shares were sold on a first-in-first-out basis. That will probably lead to a heftier tax gain. If your fund investment was successful, the shares you bought earlier probably cost you the least—so your gain (and tax) is the highest.

The second costly risk that good record-keeping will help avoid is paying tax on reinvested dividends. If you are a successful long-term fund investor, the check you receive when you finally liquidate your holdings will include a substantial sum of reinvested dividends. Each year that you held the fund, you received a year-end statement showing the value of these reinvested dividends—and you were required to report them as taxable income for the year. When you then sell fund shares, you don't have to pay taxes again on the part of your proceeds represented by reinvested dividends. But you (or your accountant) will have to figure out how much those reinvested dividends amount to by adding up the figures reported on your account statements. The fund will not do that for you.

CLOSED-END FUNDS

Closed-end funds are one of the oldest forms of pooled investment (they originated in Europe in the early nineteenth century), but remained largely unfamiliar to most individual investors until fairly recently. Suddenly, in the late 1980s, a number of new ones started up, often under the name of a star money-manager, and billions of investment dollars have since poured into them.

What Closed-End Funds Are

You can find about the same variety of closed-end funds as mutual funds—equity funds, equity funds specialized in a particular industry or country, taxable and nontaxable bond funds, etc. But the closed-end structure is quite different from that of mutual funds.

A closed-end fund makes one initial distribution of stock to raise capital to invest. After that (unlike mutual funds), shares of the closed-end fund trade on a stock exchange. You buy the shares from your broker at the initial issue or, later, via the exchange. And you sell closed-end-fund shares the same way.

This means that the value of your shares in a closed-end fund is determined by more than their net asset value. For equity funds, the market forces of supply and demand for the fund can push per-share value either under or over the net asset value.

In early 1989, for instance, shares of closed-end funds invested in Korean and Taiwanese company stocks were trading at premiums significantly over their net asset value because the funds were the only way for American investors to participate easily in the fast growth of companies in those countries. Obviously, shares of a closed-end equity fund are likely to sell above net asset value, too, if the performance of the fund's manager is outstanding.

For bond funds, still another factor influences the market price of fund shares: yield. When a bond fund's yield is above average, the market price of its shares may not drift down even though its net asset value falls because most investors in closed-end bond funds focus primarily on yield.

What You Must Know Before Making a Choice

It's important for you to know whether the shares of a closed-end fund are selling *above* net asset value (at a premium) or *below* (at a discount) but that's not the primary concern for a long-term college investor. First and foremost you must make a decision about the *kind of securities* in which the fund is invested. Are they suitable for your stage in building a college fund? Considering your tolerance for risk, are you comfortable owning those securities or with the investment strategy of the fund manager explained in the fund prospectus? Once you've decided on the type of fund that fits your goals, you can start to pay closer attention to the numbers.

When a closed-end fund is first offered on the market (which is likely to be the time you first hear about it from your broker), it will probably be priced at a premium to net asset value. The underwriter who arranges the sale has to be paid for packaging and selling the issue (the firm's fee is usually about 7%). So, for instance, you may pay $10 per share for a fund with a net asset value of $9.30 per share. Financially speaking, this has the same effect as buying a mutual fund with a front-end sales commission.

A number of things could then happen. With a successfully managed equity fund, the net asset value could soon be up to the initial offering price (IOP) and then go beyond it. With less successful management, or because the type of equities fall out of favor with the stock market, the net asset value may fall. With a bond fund, some of the difference between net asset value and the initial offering price might be made up in a couple of distributions of income. Of course, since the bond fund is invested in fixed-rate securities, it is also possible for net asset value to slide if interest rates go up.

It is quite common for the market price of closed-end funds to drift below the initial offering price after about six months or so, although this certainly depends on general market trends and on the performance of the fund. Some funds go to a premium during that period, too. In the decade ending 1988, however, closed-end stock funds sold at an average discount to net asset value of 11.8% and closed-end bond funds at an average discount to net asset value of 3.6%, according to data from Thomas J. Hertzfeld Advisors, Inc., of Miami, Florida.

How to Buy Closed-End Funds Wisely

The widening and narrowing of spreads between a fund's net asset value and its market price are of significant interest to involved traders. For most college-fund investors, however, the selection of a closed-end fund is for long-term investing. In general, they are more appropriate for Early Planners than for Late Savers.

Give priority to deciding on the kind of securities you want a fund to be invested in—securities that suit the goals of your college fund for at least three or four years. If you are ready to buy a bond fund at its initial offering, compare the anticipated distribution rate—say 8% or so, based on the initial offering price—to the return on other fixed-rate investments, including Treasuries, CDs, and tax-free municipals. Make sure you understand how the fund manager anticipates generating that return, including the quality of the bonds that will be traded and whether the fund will use special features, such as zero bonds, to achieve its goals.

If you would rather buy a closed-end fund with a track record, get help from your broker or look at the closed-end fund list in *Barron's,* which shows you the premium or discount at which the fund shares traded during the week and its current share price. You'll also often find on that same page a chart that tracks the trend of discounts of major funds, prepared by Thomas J. Hertzfeld Advisors, Inc. Get help from your broker or track the discounts yourself on funds invested in the type of securities that you've decided are right for your college fund. One guideline sometimes used to look for opportunities: The fund's discount is several points *more* than it usually is but it's *not* narrower than the average discount for similarly invested closed-end funds.

UNIT INVESTMENT TRUSTS

A unit investment trust (UIT) is an easy-to-understand investment that you can select to mature when you need cash to meet college expenses. Decision-making is far simpler than for closed-end funds and even simpler than for mutual funds. You make a one-time choice of a type of security, investment expertise, and a maturity date.

What Unit Investment Trusts Are

A unit trust is a fixed portfolio of securities put together by a securities firm. It can be a portfolio of, for instance, municipal bonds, corporate bonds, company stocks, or international securities. Generally, the securities are held in trust by a bank, which collects the interest, dividends, and principal as securities mature and distributes payments to investors.

What You Must Know Before Making a Choice

The unique features of unit investment trusts are:

- The trust has a stated maturity, generally three, five, ten, or fifteen years. At the end of that period, the securities in the trust either mature or are sold and the trust is terminated, which makes it easy for you to plan for the future.
- The portfolio is not managed. Investment professionals select the securities at the start and monitor those securities throughout the life of the trust. They are generally *not* traded as they are in either a mutual fund or closed-end fund. You know the securities in which you are investing.

Though the variety of UITs is fairly wide, it is not as expansive as the choices available in mutual funds. As you review the options listed in the Investment Guides in Part Two of this book, think about selecting a UIT for a specific type of investment—say, municipal bonds—rather than investing either in bonds directly or in a municipal bond mutual fund, especially if your tolerance for price volatility is low.

How to Buy Unit Investment Trusts Wisely

There is only one way to buy a UIT—from the securities firm that selects the securities for the portfolio or that chooses to sell a UIT created by another firm. Each UIT unit is usually priced at $1,000, and generally includes a built-in, one-time sales charge that can range from about 2% to 4.5% of the offering price of the portfolio. The price of UIT units and the sales charges can differ, however.

Because they have a relatively predictable lifetime, UITs fit nicely into a college fund. You can, for instance, invest in bond UITs with three-, five-, ten-, and fifteen-year maturities and simultaneously reduce your exposure to interest-rate risk while you gain the safety of diversification. Even greater safety is also available: Many municipal-bond UITs invest only in insured municipal bonds, which means an outside organization with a very high credit rating guarantees regularly scheduled payments of the bond's principal and interest. This insurance is now beginning to be offered, too, for UITs of corporate bonds.

Your broker will allow you to exchange one UIT investment for another for a small fee (around $15 per unit). Most securities firms also maintain a secondary market in UITs, which may allow you to sell units through the firm for their current market value. Inspect the offering prospectus carefully and ask your broker to find out what options are available before you invest or send money.

MORE INFORMATION ON FUNDS AND UITS

In the following chapters, you will find more information on how to use specific types of funds and UITs in your college savings plan.

For more general information on how mutual funds work, contact the Investment Company Institute, 1600 M Street, Washington, DC 20036.

9

Zero Bonds: Backbone Investments for College Funds

Zero bonds are rapidly becoming the backbone of many families' college funds. And with good reason. The investment return is so easy to understand.

The unique value of all zeros—Treasury zero bonds, municipal zero bonds, and zero corporate bonds—is that you can invest a specific amount today and know exactly what the investment will be worth at maturity. You lock in the current rate of interest for the long term.

What a Zero Is

The owner of a traditional coupon bond receives regular interest payments and then must reinvest that interest at whatever rate the market offers at the time. Zeros, however, pay no regular interest. In fact, they pay nothing at all until they actually mature. Rather, you buy a zero coupon security at a discount from its face value. In general, the longer the time to mature, the more substantial the discount. Your return is the difference between what you pay for the zero at the time of purchase and what you sell it for or what it pays when held to maturity.

Obviously, if interest rates go *down* while you own a zero bond, you'll do very well because you've locked in a higher rate. If rates go *up* during that period, however, you'll do worse than someone who could reinvest interest at the higher rates—but you're still sure of the rate of return you'll earn if you hold the bond to maturity.

Zeros are available now as corporate bonds, certificates of deposit, municipal bonds, and securities based on U.S. Treasury bonds. Corporate bonds, CDs, and municipals are direct obligation of their issuers. Zeros based on Treasuries, however, were initially created by investment banking firms to, as they call it, segment values. They deposit the Treasury bond in a trust with a custodial bank. At that point, the value of the bond's principal at maturity—called the "corpus"—was separated from the interest and the two parts were sold separately to different investors with different objectives. More recently, zeros have been issued directly.

What You Must Know Before Making a Choice

If you time the maturities of your zero bonds to when you expect to need the cash, zero bonds are a very handy way for you to match your child's projected college expenses with an investment that will have a *specific, predictable value at that time.*

The difference between what you pay initially for the zero bond and what you cash it in for at maturity is a true compounded rate of interest—as if that interest had actually been paid to you several times a year and you reinvested it at the same rate each time. Compound interest is a powerful engine for growth. In early 1989, for instance, you could invest about $10,000 in a Treasury zero and count on being able to cash a bond held to a five-year maturity for about $15,000, or one held to a ten-year maturity for about $24,000, or one held to a fifteen-year maturity for about $36,000. You would have been locking in interest rates of 8.8% to just over 9% on those bonds. To put that performance into the perspective of the stock market, you would achieve the same results over ten years with that $10,000 compounding at 8.8% as you would if you invested in stocks of the Dow Industrial Average when it was 2000 and the Dow then proceeded to advance to 4648 in a decade.

There's a simple and quick way to figure out how long it will take you to double your money in a zero called "the Rule of 72": Divide 72 by the rate of interest on the bond. At 8.5% a year compounded, for instance, it takes almost eight and half years; at 9%, it takes eight years. The "Rule of 72" is handy to use to make a quick comparison of what you'll get from a zero as compared to other investments you're considering at the same time.

Even though you won't actually receive the interest earned on your zeros until you sell them or they mature, the IRS correctly holds that you are really earning interest during that time. So, you are responsible for paying taxes each year on that "imputed" interest. You should consider two ways to reduce that tax liability:

1. Buy zero municipals or Treasuries. On tax-free municipal zeros, of course, you won't have a tax liability. And you pay only federal income tax but no state or local taxes on the imputed interest from your zero Treasuries.

2. Donate zeros to a Minors Trust.

Zero Treasuries and zero municipals offer protection against one of the greatest disappointments for bond investors—a decision by the bond issuer to "call" the bond, which means retiring the bond before it matures by paying bondholders a slight premium over the maturity value. Issuers are tempted to do this, of course, when interest rates drop below the rate they are paying on a bond because they can then raise money at the lower rate. Bond investors, however, lose the higher rate they thought they had locked in. The vast majority of Treasury bonds (and thus Treasury zeros) are not callable, however. And even though many regular municipal bonds *are* callable, zero municipals are generally the last bonds to be called (if they can be called at all) and the risk to investors has been quite slight over the years.

Finally, since zeros are often a long-term investment, you want to be sure the entity that issues the bond will be around to redeem it in cash when it matures. You can assume the U.S. government will be there for your Treasury zeros. You have a high degree of security, too, when you buy high-grade and insured municipal zeros. Corporate zeros, though, are riskier, since the fortunes of even the biggest companies can undergo significant change over a decade or more. Recently, however, some utility-company zeros have been insured in unit investment trusts, which means the principal and interest payments are protected.

How to Buy Zeros Wisely

At any point, your broker or bank can tell you exactly what the long-term rate of return will be on a zero bond of any maturity and exactly what you'll have at maturity, making it relatively easy to see how an investment in a zero compares to other investments at the time.

Zeros were created originally in a period of high interest rates—during the early 1980s. When interest rates then began to fall and the great bull market in stocks began, sales of zero bonds languished. In general, when investors find they can lock in rates of around 9% on Treasury zeros and around 8% on municipal zeros, they move into them. That happened in mid-1988, in the aftermath of the October 1987 stock-market crash, and represents a commonsense understanding that those rates of return are attractive over the long run.

Zeros *are* a long-term investment, most suitable for the college funds of *Early Planners* and least suitable for *Last-minute Savers.* The longer the time until the zero matures, the greater the power of compound interest. But, when you invest in a zero, you are, in fact, making a bet on the future trend of interest rates. Their simplicity, therefore, shouldn't lure you into making them the *only* investment in your college fund. If you invest substantial amounts of cash in zeros during a period of relatively low interest rates, you may not be building up the values in your college fund as effectively as possible. If interest rates then climb, you may find that too much of your assets are tied up in an illiquid investment to take advantage of the upward trend.

True, securities firms maintain a secondary market in zeros, which means you can sell them through your broker before they mature. It's wiser, though, for college-fund investors to consider zeros a buy-and-hold decision. Don't be tempted to use them to speculate on interest rates and play the bond market for capital gains. All bonds drop in value when interest rates climb, but the market value of zeros drops more sharply than that of regular bonds during these times (and climbs higher when interest rates decline).

The reason for the volatility of zeros is simple. Coupon-bond holders can ease the financial damage that rising interest rates do to the value of their bond holdings by reinvesting the interest payments they receive at those higher rates. Zero-bond holders are locked into their rates. If you tried to sell your low-interest zeros in a high-interest market before the bonds matured, the availability of a secondary market to make the sale might not protect you. Your loss, if any, would depend on how long you held the bonds and the length of time remaining to maturity. On the other hand, when interest rates *drop,* zero bonds continue to earn their higher rates. They will increase in value because regular-bond holders have to settle for reinvesting their interest payments at lower and lower rates. But, if you are tempted to sell your zeros for a gain at that point, you would face the same problem—finding a place to reinvest your proceeds at a satisfactory rate for the long term.

Appropriateness Guide

Early Planners, for whom zeros are best suited, can limit interest-rate risk on the zeros in their college funds by buying them at different maturities—say, five years, ten years, and fifteen years. Then, if interest rates rise, they can reinvest at higher rates the proceeds of the first ones to mature, making up somewhat for the relatively lower rates being earned on the longer-term zeros still in the college fund.

Zero municipals are especially useful for Early Planners in the highest tax brackets since they won't have to pay taxes on the imputed interest.

Late Starters don't have as much flexibility to protect themselves against interest-rate risk, nor do they have as much time to take advantage of the compounding effect of zeros. Therefore, Late Starters should be especially cautious about the proportion of their college fund invested in these bonds. Nevertheless, zeros are an excellent choice if interest rates are near 8% to 8.5% (the annual rate of increase in college costs at expensive schools). They are also appropriate for Late Starters who like the idea of knowing the amount they will have in a few years when the bonds mature and tuition payments are due.

More Information on Zeros

There is more information on bonds in the chapters that follow on Treasuries (Chapter 10), municipals (Chapter 12), and corporate bonds (Chapter 13).

10

U.S. Government Securities: The Treasury Benchmark and Others

The head of General Electric used to start out every review of operations at subsidiaries by announcing: "Your job is to convince me that we shouldn't put all the money we have invested in this subsidiary into government bonds." In other words, what you can earn by investing in supersafe U.S. government securities provides a useful benchmark for assessing alternative ways to invest the money in your college fund.

What U.S. Treasury Securities Are

The credit risk on Treasury securities is zero: The federal government has never defaulted on any of its obligations. (Although Treasury zeros are not issued by the U.S. Treasury, they are collateralized by Treasury securities and are considered to be as safe. See Chapter Nine for details.) Because Treasuries have what is called "the full faith and credit of the U.S. government" behind them—the highest credit rating in the world—Treasury bonds, notes, and bills generally offer a lower yield than other securities of the same maturity.

Treasuries come in three units:

• *Bills* (known as T-bills), which have the shortest maturity—up to one year when first issued by the Treasury.

• *Notes,* which range in maturity from two to ten years when first issued.

• *Bonds,* which have a maturity of ten to thirty years when first issued.

The Treasury has a regular schedule of issuing new bills, notes, and bonds as it refinances maturing debt or accumulates additional debt. This schedule is listed in the table below:

WHAT U.S. SECURITIES ARE SOLD WHEN

UNIT	MINIMUM YOU CAN BUY	WHEN SOLD
TREASURY BILLS	$10,000 minimum; in increments of $5,000 after the initial $10,000	First business day of each week
TREASURY NOTES	$5,000 minimum for two- or three-year notes	Two-year note at end of each month Three-year note in mid-February, May, August, November
	$1,000 minimum for notes or bonds of four years or more	Four-year note at end of March, June, September, December Five-year note in early March, June, September, December Seven-year note in early January, April, July, October
TREASURY BONDS	$1,000 minimum	Ten-year and thirty-year bond in mid-February, May, August, November

What You Must Know Before Making a Choice

Though your actual interest and principal on Treasuries are not at risk, you can lose money on this type of investment. There's inflation risk. During much of the 1970s, the interest rate paid by the U.S.

government lagged behind the inflation rate. Investors who held on to Treasuries (and other bonds) bought early in the decade certainly were paid off eventually, but with much depreciated dollars. And there's market risk, too. Investors who sold their 7% Treasuries when interest rates began to escalate into double digits took a loss on the value of the securities.

Nevertheless, it's a good idea for you to stay abreast of what you can get on Treasury issues because of their value as a yardstick. How much higher is the return on other investments? Is that anticipated return high enough to make you feel comfortable with the additional level of risk?

The interest earned on Treasury securities is exempt from state and local income taxes (since local governments can't tax the federal government) but *is* subject to federal income tax. Remember, therefore, that you need a higher yield on a fully taxable investment to wind up with the same after-tax return.

The following three charts illustrate how the yield spreads between long-term Treasury bonds and Government National Mortgage Association mortgage-backed securities, municipals and high-grade corporate bonds narrowed and widened between the summer of 1987 and the spring of 1989.

CHANGES IN THE YIELD SPREAD BETWEEN LONG-TERM TREASURY BONDS AND GNMAS, HIGH-GRADE MUNICIPALS, AND HIGH-GRADE CORPORATE BONDS OF SIMILAR MATURITIES (AUGUST 1987–FEBRUARY 1989)

Treasuries and GNMAs

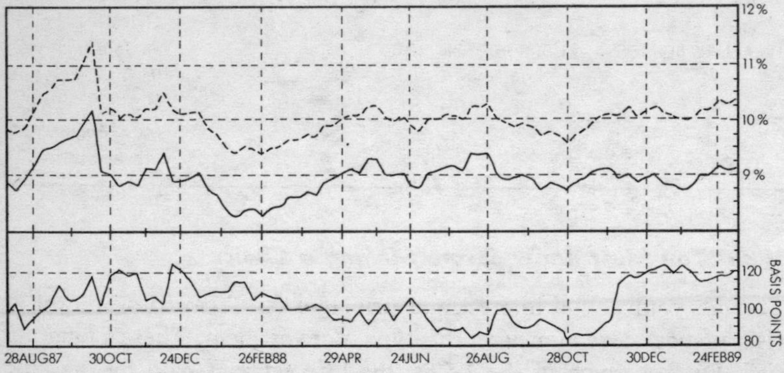

See caption on facing page.

The top line (broken) shows how yields on GNMA (Ginnie Mae) mortgage-backed securities generally hover about one percentage point above the yields on long-term Treasuries (solid line just below). The line at the bottom traces the difference between GNMA and Treasury yields during this period in basis points (100 basis points equals one percentage point). It illustrates how the difference in yield (the spread) between the two types of securities tended to stay in a range between 80 basis points (0.80 of a percentage point) and 120 basis points (1.2 percentage points) even though this period covers the bull market in stocks through August 1987, the October 1987 crash, subsequent recovery, and the general increase in interest rates that started in late 1988.

Treasuries and Municipals

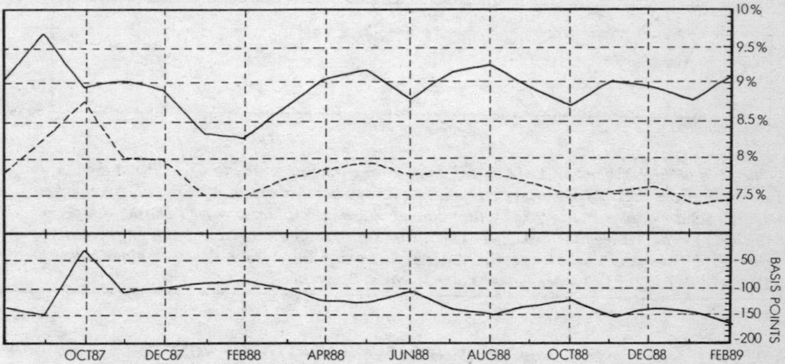

Municipals (broken line) generally yield less than Treasuries (solid line at the top). The chart clearly shows, however, that in the period immediately after the October 1987 stock market crash, investor concern about "safety" created such demand for Treasury securities that yields on governments dropped very close to those on municipals. When the spread is that narrow, municipals are considered "cheap" since municipal-bond income is tax-exempt while federal income tax is due on Treasury bond interest. In subsequent months the spread widened as yields on municipals drifted down because demand continued high and the supply of new issues on the market was tight. By the time the spread was above 1.6 percentage points in February 1989, municipals were considered "rich," which means relatively expensive in relation to Treasury issues.

Treasuries and High-grade Corporates

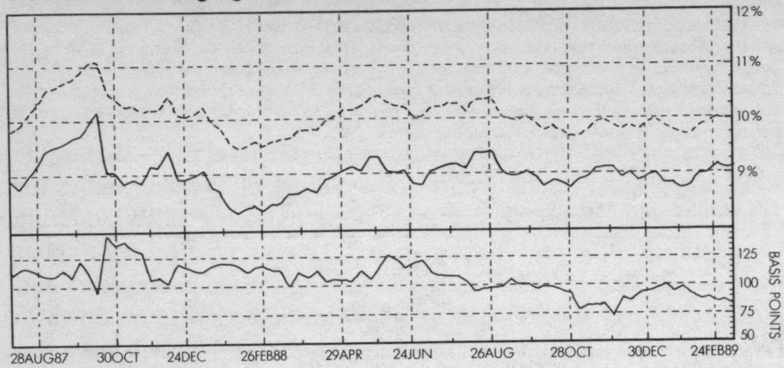

The yield on high-grade (AAA/AA rated), long-term corporate bonds (broken line at the top) is generally above that of Treasuries (solid line just below) because corporates are fully taxable and Treasuries are only partially taxable (in addition to being considered safer). During this period the yield spread between the two types of securities (third line) averaged just over one percentage point (100 basis points equals one percentage point) and ranged from 1.45 percentage points in October 1987 to 0.73 of a percentage point in early December 1988.

Data and charts from Bloomberg L.P., 499 Park Avenue, New York, NY 10022. Used with permission. The information was obtained from sources which Bloomberg and its suppliers believe reliable, but they do not guarantee its accuracy.

This is the formula that will tell you what the equivalent yield on a fully taxable investment must be to match that on a Treasury:

$$\frac{\text{Interest rate on government security } \mathbf{(A)}}{1.00 - (\text{your highest state income tax bracket} + \text{your local income tax rate}) \ \mathbf{(B)}} = \mathbf{(C)}$$

Suppose, for instance:

(A) You were able to get a 7.8% (0.078) rate on a Treasury.

(B) The highest bracket into which you fell on your state's income tax was 7% (0.07) and you faced a local income tax of 1% (0.01), for a total of 8% (0.08). Then, 1.00 – 0.08 = 0.092.

(C) On your calculator: A (0.078) ÷ B (0.092) = C (0.0847) or 8.47%.

Conclusion: You would need an 8.47% return on a fully taxable investment to contribute as much to your college fund as you would earn on a 7.8% Treasury security.

How to Buy Treasuries Wisely

There is a simple technique to minimize your market risk—that is, the effect of changing interest rates—on holdings of Treasury issues (or any other fixed-interest securities). The technique is called laddering (or stepping). Buy your Treasuries so that you wind up with about one-tenth of your holdings in bonds that mature about ten years out, another tenth in bonds maturing nine years out, and so on down to Treasury bills with a one-year or shorter duration. This will leave you with an overall maturity of about five years. A somewhat simpler version would be to take larger "steps," dividing your Treasury holdings into thirds, for instance or some similar mix. As each step in the ladder matures, you reinvest the proceeds in Treasuries of a maturity that extends your laddered portfolio. For instance, if you start with a mix of two, four, six and eight-year maturities, you would buy another eight-year Treasury when your two-year note matures. Then, as you get closer to the end of building your college fund, reinvest in shorter and shorter maturities—matching the time when you will have to cash in the investments.

Rolling over fixed-interest issues this way is almost a kind of dollar-cost averaging on interest rates. If the general trend of rates rises, you're adding in securities that pay a higher rate of return. If rates decline, your new additions will be at a lower rate but remaining issues in the college fund are earning at their higher rates.

Laddering is particularly effective only if you hold your Treasuries to maturity, which is an appropriate strategy for most college-fund building.

You can select Treasury issues to ladder either from new issues or from the so-called secondary market, where securities issued in the past are bought and sold. Trading in the secondary bond markets is reported in every issue of *The Wall Street Journal* (listed under "Treasury Bonds, Notes & Bills"), on the financial pages of some daily newspapers, and weekly in *Barron's.*

The Wall Street Journal's list for trading on January 3, 1989, prepared from data provided by Bloomberg Financial Markets, New York, is reproduced on page 116.

TREASURY BONDS, NOTES & BILLS

Tuesday January 3, 1989

Representative Over-the-Counter quotations based on transactions of $1 million or more as of 4 p.m. Eastern time.

Hyphens in bid-and-asked and bid changes represent 32nds; 101-01 means 101 1/32. a-Plus 1/64. b-Yield to call date. d-Minus 1/64. k-Nonresident aliens exempt from withholding taxes. n-Treasury notes. p-Treasury note; nonresident aliens exempt from withholding taxes.

. Source: Bloomberg Financial Markets

TREASURY BONDS AND NOTES

Rate	Mat. Date	Bid	Asked	Bid Chg.	Yld.
6⅛	1989 Jan p	99-25	99-29	....	7.22
14⅝	1989 Jan n	100-02	100-06	-04	7.80
8	1989 Feb p	99-28	100	....	7.76
6¼	1989 Feb p	99-20	99-24	+03	7.75
11⅜	1989 Feb n	100-07	100-11	-01	7.99
11¼	1989 Mar p	100-17	100-21	....	8.18
6⅜	1989 Mar p	99-14	99-18	....	8.13
7⅛	1989 Apr p	99-14	99-18	+01	8.42
14⅜	1989 Apr n	101-17	101-21	-04	8.02
6⅞	1989 May p	99-08	99-12	....	8.57
9¼	1989 May n	100-01	100-07	-01	8.52
8	1989 May p	99-19	99-23	....	8.65
11¾	1989 May n	101	101-04	....	8.41
7⅜	1989 Jun p	99-09	99-13	....	8.63
9⅝	1989 Jun p	100-11	100-15	+01	8.62
7⅝	1989 Jul p	99-07	99-11	+01	8.80
14½	1989 Jul n	102-25	102-29	-05	8.75
7¾	1989 Aug p	99-05	99-09	+02	8.88
6⅝	1989 Aug p	98-17	98-21	+01	8.90
13⅞	1989 Aug n	102-24	102-28	-02	8.91
8½	1989 Sep k	99-16	99-20	+02	9.00
9⅜	1989 Sep p	100-04	100-08	+02	8.98
11⅞	1989 Oct n	101-30	102-02	-01	9.02
7⅞	1989 Oct p	99	99-04	....	8.98
6⅜	1989 Nov p	97-23	97-27	+01	9.01
10¾	1989 Nov n	101-07	101-11	-02	9.06
12¾	1989 Nov p	102-29	103-01	-02	8.98
7¾	1989 Nov p	98-25	98-29	-02	9.02
7⅞	1989 Dec p	98-23	98-27	-02	9.12
8⅜	1989 Dec p	99-10	99-14	-01	8.98
7⅜	1990 Jan k	98-04	98-08	-01	9.11
10½	1990 Jan n	101-07	101-11	....	9.10
3½	1990 Feb	94-15	95-01	....	8.25
6½	1990 Feb k	97-04	97-08	....	9.14
7⅛	1990 Feb k	97-22	97-26	....	9.15
11	1990 Feb p	101-24	101-28	-02	9.17
7¼	1990 Mar p	97-20	97-24	-02	9.20
7⅜	1990 Mar p	97-25	97-29	....	9.19
10½	1990 Apr n	101-12	101-16	-05	9.20
7⅜	1990 Apr p	97-30	98-02	-04	9.20
7⅞	1990 May k	98-08	98-12	....	9.16
8¼	1990 May	98-28	99-02	-05	8.96
8⅛	1990 May p	98-15	98-19	-04	9.20
11⅜	1990 May p	102-19	102-23	-02	9.19
7¼	1990 Jun p	97-08	97-12	-02	9.17
8	1990 Jun p	98-08	98-12	-03	9.19
10¾	1990 Jul n	102-01	102-05	-04	9.20
8⅜	1990 Jul p	98-22	98-26	-04	9.19
7⅞	1990 Aug k	97-29	98-01	-02	9.20
9⅞	1990 Aug p	100-27	100-31	-02	9.20
10¾	1990 Aug n	102-04	102-08	-06	9.20
8⅜	1990 Aug	99	99-04	-03	9.19
6¾	1990 Sep p	95-29	96-01	-13	9.26
8½	1990 Sep p	98-23	98-27	-02	9.22
11½	1990 Oct n	103-16	103-20	-01	9.22
8¼	1990 Oct p	98-08	98-12	-05	9.23
8	1990 Nov p	97-27	97-31	-03	9.20
9⅝	1990 Nov k	100-17	100-21	-05	9.22
13	1990 Nov n	106-05	106-09	-06	9.23
8⅞	1990 Nov p	99-13	99-17	-03	9.14
6⅝	1990 Dec p	95-10	95-14	-04	9.19
11¾	1991 Jan n	104-17	104-21	-03	9.18
7⅜	1991 Feb p	96-14	96-18	-05	9.19
9⅛	1991 Feb k	99-22	99-26	-06	9.21
6¾	1991 Mar p	94-30	95-02	-04	9.23
12⅜	1991 Apr n	106-06	106-10	-06	9.22
8⅛	1991 May p	97-20	97-24	-04	9.20
14½	1991 May n	111-21	111-25	-07	8.85
7⅞	1991 Jun n	96-31	97-03	-04	9.21
13¾	1991 Jul n	109-28	110	-07	9.22
7½	1991 Aug p	95-31	96-03	-03	9.21
8¾	1991 Aug p	98-25	98-29	-04	9.22
14⅞	1991 Aug n	113-13	113-17	-07	8.94
9⅛	1991 Sep k	99-20	99-24	-06	9.22
12¼	1991 Oct p	107-03	107-07	-10	9.23
6½	1991 Nov p	93-03	93-07	-07	9.24
8½	1991 Nov p	98-02	98-06	-07	9.23
14¼	1991 Nov n	113-02	113-06	-07	8.92
8¼	1991 Dec k	97-12	97-16	-06	9.23
11⅝	1992 Jan p	106-01	106-05	-06	9.25
6⅝	1992 Feb p	92-29	93-01	-05	9.25
14⅝	1992 Feb n	114-20	114-24	-07	9.07
7⅞	1992 Mar p	96-01	96-05	-11	9.27
11¾	1992 Apr	106-24	106-28	-07	9.26
6⅝	1992 May k	92-13	92-17	-08	9.26
13¾	1992 May n	112-16	112-20	-10	9.28
8¼	1992 Jun p	96-30	97-02	-09	9.25
10⅜	1992 Jul p	103-07	103-11	-07	9.24
4¼	1987-92 Aug	94-15	95-01	-02	5.79
7¼	1992 Aug	93-23	94-01	-14	9.22
8¼	1992 Aug p	96-29	97-01	-05	9.23
8¾	1992 Sep p	98-10	98-14	-09	9.25
9¾	1992 Oct p	101-13	101-17	-09	9.25
8⅜	1992 Nov p	97-03	97-07	-07	9.24
10½	1992 Nov n	103-27	103-31	-10	9.25
8¾	1993 Jan p	98-06	98-10	-11	9.26
4	1988-93 Feb	94-15	95-01	-02	5.36
6¾	1993 Feb	91-12	91-30	-14	9.14
7⅞	1993 Feb	95-11	95-16	-14	9.21
8¼	1993 Feb p	96-15	96-19	-09	9.26
10⅞	1993 Feb n	105-09	105-13	-07	9.26
7⅜	1993 Apr p	93-09	93-13	-10	9.27
7⅜	1993 May	94-01	94-05	-09	9.28
10⅛	1993 May n	102-24	102-28	-12	9.30
7¼	1993 Jul p	92-18	92-22	-10	9.26
7½	1988-93 Aug	93-07	93-13	-12	9.29
8⅝	1993 Aug	97-20	97-28	-12	9.20
8¾	1993 Aug p	97-31	98-03	-14	9.26
11⅞	1993 Aug n	109-11	109-15	-18	9.30
7⅛	1993 Oct p	91-21	91-25	-10	9.29
8⅝	1993 Nov	97-31	98-05	-12	9.10
11¾	1993 Nov n	109-11	109-15	-12	9.28
9	1993 Nov p	99-01	99-05	-12	9.20
7	1994 Jan p	90-26	90-30	-10	9.30
9	1994 Feb	99-07	99-11	-13	9.16
8⅞	1994 Feb p	98-13	98-17	-13	9.22
7	1994 Apr p	90-15	90-19	-12	9.29
4⅛	1989-94 May	94-15	95-01	-04	5.20
13⅛	1994 May p	115-23	115-27	-13	9.30
8	1994 Jul n	94-12	94-16	-13	9.29
8¾	1994 Aug	98-21	98-29	-12	9.00
12⅝	1994 Aug p	114-06	114-10	-13	9.29
9½	1994 Oct k	100-26	100-30	-10	9.28
10⅛	1994 Nov	103-18	103-22	-14	9.29
11⅝	1994 Nov	110-04	110-08	-16	9.31
8⅝	1995 Jan p	96-25	96-29	-14	9.31
3	1995 Feb	94-16	95-02	-03	3.92
10½	1995 Feb	105-09	105-13	-19	9.32
11¼	1995 Feb p	108-24	108-28	-13	9.31
8⅜	1995 Apr p	95-16	95-20	-14	9.31
10⅜	1995 May	104-28	105	-19	9.31
11¼	1995 May p	109	109-04	-15	9.31
12⅝	1995 May	115-16	115-20	-25	9.31
8⅞	1995 Jul p	97-30	98-02	-09	9.28
10½	1995 Aug p	105-20	105-24	-15	9.31
8⅝	1995 Oct p	96-22	96-26	-16	9.26
9½	1995 Nov p	100-27	100-31	-16	9.30
11½	1995 Nov	110-29	111-01	-16	9.29
8⅞	1996 Feb p	97-21	97-25	-15	9.30
7⅜	1996 May p	89-23	89-27	-14	9.31
7¼	1996 Nov p	88-19	88-23	-14	9.30
8⅝	1997 Aug k	95-30	96-02	-17	9.30
8½	1997 May k	95-13	95-17	-14	9.28
8⅞	1997 Nov p	97-15	97-19	-16	9.28
8⅛	1998 Feb p	93-02	93-06	-14	9.24
9	1998 May p	98-13	98-17	-15	9.23
9¼	1998 Aug p	99-31	100-03	-15	9.23
7	1993-98 May	86-14	86-18	-17	9.17
3½	1998 Nov	94-17	95-03	-02	4.11
8⅞	1998 Nov p	97-22	97-26	-17	9.21
8½	1994-99 May	94-29	95-01	-14	9.25
7⅞	1995-00 Feb	90-10	90-14	-17	9.27
8⅜	1995-00 Aug	93-16	93-20	-21	9.28
11¾	2001 Feb	117-26	118	-30	9.25
13⅛	2001 May	127-28	128-02	-30	9.26
8	1996-01 Aug	91-11	91-17	-30	9.14
13⅜	2001 Aug	129-30	130-04	-30	9.27
15¾	2001 Nov	149-18	149-24	-30	9.10
14¼	2002 Feb	138-13	138-19	-25	9.14
11⅝	2002 Nov	118-09	118-15	-25	9.23
10¾	2003 Feb	111-18	111-24	-26	9.24
10¾	2003 May	111-18	111-24	-24	9.25
11⅛	2003 Aug	114-20	114-26	-26	9.25
11⅞	2003 Nov	120-24	120-30	-29	9.25
12⅜	2004 May	125-04	125-10	-27	9.25
13¾	2004 Aug	137	137-06	-27	9.21
11⅝	2004 Nov k	119-18	119-24	-27	9.23
8¼	2000-05 May	91-13	91-19	-27	9.25
12	2005 May k	123-07	123-13	-27	9.20
10¾	2005 Aug k	112-18	112-24	-31	9.23
9⅜	2006 Feb k	101-17	101-23	-1-00	9.17
7⅝	2002-07 Feb	85-28	86-02	-28	9.22
7⅞	2002-07 Nov	87-26	88	-28	9.23
8⅜	2003-08 Aug	91-30	92-04	-28	9.25
8¾	2003-08 Nov	95-08	95-14	-29	9.25
9⅛	2004-09 May	98-22	98-28	-29	9.25
10⅜	2004-09 Nov	108-21	108-27	-31	9.30
11¾	2005-10 Feb	120-02	120-08	-28	9.30
10	2005-10 May	105-24	105-30	-31	9.28
12¾	2005-10 Nov	128-31	129-05	-31	9.29
13⅞	2006-11 May	139	139-06	-1-00	9.28
14	2006-11 Nov	140-16	140-22	-1-02	9.29
10⅜	2007-12 Nov	109-13	109-19	-30	9.29
12	2008-13 Aug	124-03	124-09	-1-00	9.29
13¼	2009-14 May	136	136-06	-1-00	9.26
12½	2009-14 Aug k	129-07	129-13	-1-00	9.27
11¾	2009-14 Nov k	123-03	123-09	-1-00	9.22
11¼	2015 Feb k	120-25	120-31	-1-00	9.13
10⅝	2015 Aug k	114-25	114-31	-1-00	9.12
9⅞	2015 Nov	107-07	107-13	-1-00	9.13
9¼	2016 Feb k	101	101-06	-1-00	9.13
7¼	2016 May k	81-06	81-12	-27	9.11
7½	2016 Nov k	83-22	83-28	-28	9.10
8¾	2017 May k	96-07	96-13	-31	9.10
8⅞	2017 Aug k	97-14	97-20	-1-00	9.11
9⅛	2018 May k	100-02	100-08	-27	9.10
9	2018 Nov	98-31	99-05	-31	9.08

U.S. TREASURY BILLS

Mat. date	Bid (Discount)	Asked (Discount)	Yield
-1989-			
1- 5	5.51	3.49	3.54
1-12	5.51	4.49	6.56
1-19	6.16	5.64	5.73
1-26	6.01	5.49	5.58
2- 2	6.96	6.44	6.56
2- 9	7.40	7.28	7.44
2-16	7.50	7.43	7.60
2-23	7.50	7.43	7.61
3- 2	7.92	7.85	8.06
3- 9	7.98	7.94	8.17
3-16	8.14	8.10	8.35
3-23	8.11	8.07	8.33
3-30	8.15	8.11	8.38
4- 6	8.23	8.19	8.48
4-13	8.23	8.19	8.50
4-20	8.30	8.26	8.58
4-27	8.19	8.15	8.48
5- 4	8.23	8.19	8.54
5-11	8.27	8.23	8.59
5-18	8.28	8.24	8.62
5-25	8.25	8.21	8.60
6- 1	8.25	8.21	8.61
6- 8	8.34	8.30	8.73
6-15	8.29	8.22	8.65
6-22	8.27	8.23	8.68
6-29	8.29	8.25	8.72
7- 6	8.37	8.33	8.82
8- 3	8.45	8.41	8.92
8-31	8.43	8.39	8.91
9-28	8.44	8.40	8.96
10-26	8.48	8.45	9.05
11-24	8.46	8.42	9.06
12-21	8.43	8.39	9.07

As you look at the top of the "Treasury Bonds, Notes & Bills" list, you'll find issues with the most recent maturity dates (the date is under columns headed "Mat. Date"). Maturities down the list stretch out all the way to "the long bond"—the bond due thirty years hence, the Treasury's longest maturity.

Look down the list until you find the range of maturities you're looking for—say, five, ten, or fifteen years out. Now check the yield in the extreme right-hand column. What you'll earn if you buy that bond will probably be somewhat less than that figure because you'll buy it at a slightly higher price than the "asked" price. (The "bid" and "asked" prices are for big transactions by professional bond traders, who presumably settle on a price between the two numbers.)

That yield, you'll note, is generally different from the rate in the extreme left-hand column—the interest rate set on the bond at the time it was originally issued. When the yield on a bond is *lower* than the rate listed for that same bond, you'll usually find that bid and asked prices are both over 100. That means you would have to pay a premium over the face value of the bond ($1,000) to buy it. If the asked price is 103.31, the price of the bond would be at least $1,033.10 (probably more for an individual buyer)—a premium of $33.10 per $1,000 face-value bond. If the yield for a bond is *higher* than the rate, the asked price will generally be less than 100, which means the bond is selling at a discount, or less than $1,000 per bond. (An asked price of 95.01 means $9,501 per bond.)

Bonds sold at a premium are not "expensive," and bonds sold at a discount are not a "bargain." The daily trading in bonds simply adjusts the relationship between the price of the bond to its fixed interest rate as market interest rates change. If the fixed rate on the Treasury that has about two years until maturity (say, the 11¾% that matures in January 1991) is higher than what the Treasury currently has to pay to sell a new two-year Treasury note, this older issue sells at a premium price. If you purchased that bond at a premium price of about $1,042, you'd collect interest at an annual rate of 11¾% per year on a face value of $1,000 and you'd get only $1,000 for the bond when it matured in two years. So your actual yield to maturity turns out to be just over 9%.

If Treasuries of the right maturity to ladder in your college fund appear to be available at a satisfactory yield, ask your broker or banker to give you a quote on specific bonds in that category. You'll be told the price you'd have to pay for the bonds and the yield to maturity you'd get.

Keep in mind that you'll now be receiving a stream of interest payments on the bond every six months that you'll have to *reinvest.* Your broker can probably arrange to have the interest payments flow directly into a money-market account. If you elect to receive the payments directly, or have them flow directly into your bank checking account from the Treasury, make sure you spend the income only on college expenses. If you're still at the stage of building up your college fund, you *must* reinvest it promptly.

The Treasury will now set up a Direct Account for you to use to buy new Treasury securities. This makes it very easy to invest directly—and to reinvest proceeds automatically as bills mature. You're free to terminate your reinvestment instructions at any time if you decide alternative short-term investments are better for you.

You can call or write your local Federal Reserve Bank (see Appendix A for addresses and phone numbers) for an application to open a Treasury Direct Account. Usually, however, the quickest and easiest way is to set up the account at the time you buy a T-bill, note, or bond from the Treasury.

Simply call or write the local Federal Reserve Bank for a "tender," such as the one reproduced on the following page, which is the form used to purchase a 26-week Treasury bill.

Under "Automatic Reinvestment" at the bottom of the Tender Form, circle the number of times the proceeds should be reinvested. Once the form and your check to buy new bills is accepted, you'll have an account in the Treasury Direct Book-entry Securities System.

That Direct Account can also be used to buy new issues of Treasury bonds and notes as they become available. You'll receive regular statements of all transactions in your account. And all interest payments from your Treasury investments are transferred electronically to a bank savings or checking account that you specify. (You cannot receive the interest payments by check mailed to your home.) A Treasury Direct Account is a simple and inexpensive way to keep track of the Treasury portion of your college fund.

If you want to sell any of these Treasury securities *before* they mature, however, or need to use them as collateral for a loan, you will have to instruct the Treasury to transfer your assets to an account at your broker or commercial bank and then sell them.

What Ginnie Maes Are

Congress has authorized several agencies to raise money from the public to provide credit for the housing market, agriculture, and other special sectors of the economy. Many of these securities are supported

FORM PD 5176-2
(January 1988)

OMB No. 1535-0069
Expires: 01-31-89

TREASURY DIRECT

TENDER FOR 26-WEEK TREASURY BILL

ENDER INFORMATION

AMOUNT OF TENDER: $ ______

BID TYPE (Check One) ☐ NONCOMPETITIVE ☐ COMPETITIVE AT ___ . ___ %

CCOUNT NUMBER ___ - ___ - ___

INVESTOR INFORMATION

ACCOUNT NAME

ADDRESS

CITY STATE ZIP CODE

AXPAYER IDENTIFICATION NUMBER

1ST NAMED OWNER ___ - ___ - ___ SOCIAL SECURITY NUMBER OR ___ - ___ EMPLOYER IDENTIFICATION NUMBER

ELEPHONE NUMBERS

WORK ( ) - HOME ( ) -

AYMENT ATTACHED

TOTAL PAYMENT: $ ______

CASH (01): $ ______ CHECKS (02/03): $ ______

SECURITIES (05): $ ______ $ ______

OTHER (06): $ ______ $ ______

FOR DEPARTMENT USE

TENDER NUMBER

912794

CUSIP

ISSUE DATE

RECEIVED BY

DATE RECEIVED

EXT REG ☐

FOREIGN ☐

BACKUP ☐

REVIEW ☐

CLASS ☐

NUMBERS

IRECT DEPOSIT INFORMATION

ROUTING NUMBER

FINANCIAL INSTITUTION NAME

ACCOUNT NUMBER

ACCOUNT NAME

ACCOUNT TYPE (Check One) ☐ CHECKING ☐ SAVINGS

UTOMATIC REINVESTMENT

1 2 3 4 Circle the number of sequential 26-week reinvestments you want to schedule at this time

UTHORIZATION

For the notice required under the Privacy and Paperwork Reduction Acts, see the accompanying instructions.

I submit this tender pursuant to the provisions of Department of the Treasury Circulars, Public Debt Series Nos. 1-86 and 2-86 and the public announcement issued by the Department of the Treasury.

Under penalties of perjury, I certify that the number shown on this form is my correct taxpayer identification number and that I am not subject to backup withholding because (1) I have not been notified that I am subject to backup withholding as a result of a failure to report all interest or dividends, or (2) the Internal Revenue Service has notified me that I am no longer subject to backup withholding. I further certify that all other information provided on this form is true, correct and complete.

SIGNATURE ______ DATE ______

by the credit of the U.S. government, though not all are fully backed. The general impression of the investment community, however, is that it would be very unlikely for the federal government to allow any of these agencies to default on its securities. Agency securities generally offer investors a slightly higher yield over Treasuries with little sacrifice in risk or quality.

The most widely known of these issues are the mortgage-backed securities issued by the Government National Mortgage Association (called "Ginnie Maes" for GNMA). Each Ginnie Mae certificate represents a share in a pool of mortgage loans put together by a mortgage banker, commercial bank, or savings-and-loan. The U.S. government guarantees timely payment of interest and principal.

What You Must Know Before Making a Choice

Taking advantage of the extra yield Ginnie Maes offer, however, may not be suitable for every college-fund saver. The problem is that the certificates pay a monthly stream of *both* interest income and principal. The monthly payments must then be reinvested to continue building up the assets of your college fund. Beware of investing in Ginnie Maes if you anticipate having trouble reinvesting the monthly flow of income or your savings discipline and record-keeping are a bit shaky. One easy solution when you buy Ginnie Maes through a broker that also handles your fund investments is to have the monthly checks swept into a money-market fund.

A second problem for some investors is that the minimum investment in a Ginnie Mae could be around $25,000—although older certificates, where some of the principal has already been paid down, are available from brokers for less.

That doesn't mean, however, that college-fund investors have to forgo the somewhat higher yields available on Ginnie Maes and the securities issued by other agencies, such as Fannie Maes from the Federal National Mortgage Association. You must either discipline yourself to reinvest the monthly income or you can buy them through mutual funds.

How to Buy Ginnie Maes Wisely

Explain to your broker that you want a Ginnie Mae for a long-term investment. Beware of certificates selling at a premium that promise a yield well above current mortgage rates (especially when the trend in rates is downward). Under those circumstances, chances are good that many homeowners will refinance their high-interest mortgages. You could wind up getting an unusually high flow of principal back in your monthly checks and find that the value of the Ginnie Mae declines sharply and the stream of earnings you anticipated is considerably shorter.

Funds for Governments

A number of mutual funds invest in Treasuries, Ginnie Maes, and securities issued by other federal agencies. The mixture is designed to produce a yield above that of Treasuries alone. You can also find funds with portfolios concentrated in U.S. Treasuries, in GNMA securities, or even in short-term government bonds.

Instead of buying Treasuries and using the laddering technique to minimize interest-rate risk, therefore, you may prefer to diversify simply by buying shares in a government or GNMA mutual fund, leaving the task of sorting out maturities to the managers of the fund.

What You Must Know Before Making a Choice

Investing in a GNMA fund or a fund that invests in both Ginnie Maes and other federal-agency issues solves both the problem of minimum investment ($500 is the typical minimum investment in a fund) and reinvestment of proceeds (the fund will reinvest in more GNMAs).

Government funds differ in the degree to which they use various devices such as call options, puts, or futures in managing their portfolios. The techniques are designed to guard the value of bonds in the portfolio against the risk of interest-rate swings, but their effectiveness is still not certain. In general, buying a fund with a relatively "plain vanilla" approach, which means a very limited use of options and a variety of maturities, comes close to achieving what laddering does. If the managers turn out to be particularly savvy about forecasting interest rates, their results could be better.

How to Buy Government and Ginnie Mae Funds Wisely

All funds that advertise yields and returns now use a standard set of performance figures. The same data are included in the prospectus for the bond fund that the fund or your broker will furnish before you make an investment decision.

The basic figure is called *thirty-day yield.* That means the income per share actually generated by the securities in the fund over that period.

Total return is the other useful figure. Each fund must list its return for the past one-, five-, and ten-year periods, or for the life of the fund if it hasn't been around for five or ten years. That makes it easy to compare performance between funds. Total return takes into account the value of the securities in the fund as well as the income. The values may increase or decrease as interest rates change.

This uniform method of presenting investment results to investors replaces a more haphazard array of figures, including distribution rates and current yield, and quirky time periods that usually put the advertised fund in the best light but made it difficult to compare performance between different funds.

These uniform standards for reporting total return also make it easy to make fair comparisons between different Ginnie Mae funds, which used to be more difficult. Some funds accumulated substantial amounts of premium-priced Ginnie Maes with high-rate mortgages because they then were able to advertise high yields. The problem that developed for investors, however, as interest rates declined was that homeowners prepaid their high-rate mortgages and refinanced at lower rates. Since the high-rate GNMA certificates then had a much shorter life than anticipated, the premiums paid for them often weren't justified. The Securities and Exchange Commission's new rules on calculating yields reflect any anticipated losses to value from early repayments.

The SEC requires funds to use the thirty-day yield figures and the one-, five-, and ten-year figures in all ads or prospectuses. But it doesn't prohibit the funds from using other figures when talking directly with customers. So, if you're getting information over the phone from a fund, be sure to ask for the SEC thirty-day yield figures and the SEC total-return figures so you'll have what you need to make valid comparisons.

Appropriateness Guide

Early Planners: The return on long-term government bonds would have come close to matching college inflation in the first half of the 1970s. And the superb return on these bonds in 1982–86, as interest rates plummeted and the value of the bonds soared, far outpaced the increase in college costs during those four years. But the record over twenty years, from 1967 to 1986, leaves a gap between the two: a 6.9% annual return for government bonds vs. an 8.2% increase in college costs, according to a study prepared by John D. Finnerty of the College Savings Bank for a Brookings Institution Public Policy Discussion.

This suggests that even parents whose tolerance for risk is very low shouldn't rely entirely on government issues in building a college fund.

Stay alert, however, to rates offered on governments as a benchmark for making investment choices. With college expenses currently averaging about an 8%–8.5% annual increase, investing in these securities when they are available at yields around that level is a reasonable choice for those with a low tolerance for risk in building their college funds. Remember, though, if you keep your fund invested in a high proportion of fixed-interest securities, to ladder the maturities to minimize interest-rate risk.

Late Starters: When the difference in rates between shorter-term Treasury issues and longer-term issues is insignificant, the shorter-term issues can be an excellent college-fund investment choice for safety-minded parents who soon face the need for maximum liquidity to pay college expenses. Buy governments that mature about the time you need the cash.

Traditionally, shorter-term bond issues offer lower rates and longer-term issues higher rates, since the owner of a long-term bond faces interest-rate risk over a lengthier time stretch. On a graph, such as in the illustration below, with interest rates plotted vertically along the left and time plotted horizontally along the bottom, the

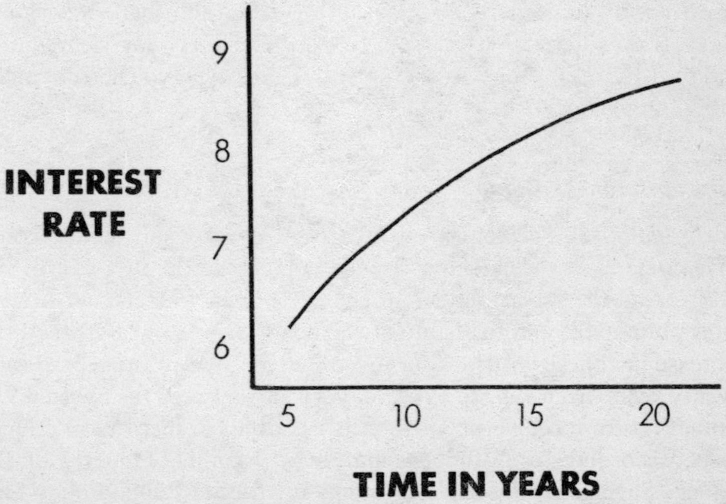

rates would trace a line sloping upward from the lower left to the upper right.

That's a traditional "yield curve." As the difference between short- and long-term rates narrows, the slope of the yield curve becomes less steep; experts call it "flat." Late Starters with a low tolerance for risk, though, might find a flattened yield curve an opportunity to stock their college funds with nice-yielding government issues scheduled to mature when they need the cash.

Rates on three-year Treasury notes actually moved *higher* than those on ten-year Treasuries ten times from 1953 to early 1989. This is what the experts call an "inverted" yield curve and is generally taken as a signal of great uncertainty ahead. For Late Starters, though, it, too, could be an investment opportunity.

Last-minute Savers should limit government-issue investments to T-bills or a short-term government unit investment trust. Compare returns on Treasury bills to those available on bank certificates of deposit and money-market funds and accounts. If the T-bill rate is relatively attractive, consider starting a Treasury Direct Account or buy the bills through your broker.

11

U.S. Savings Bonds: A Whole New Twist to an Old Way to Save for College

Ever since the U.S. government improved the return on Series EE savings bonds to enable them to compete more effectively against other financial products, they have been a convenient way to save small sums systematically for a college fund. Now Congress has made these savings bonds even more attractive for college investing—starting in January 1990.

Interest on Series EE savings bonds has always been exempt from state and local taxes, and it's been possible to defer federal income tax until the bonds are cashed. Some parents will now also be able to *avoid federal income taxes as well* on savings bonds bought from January 1, 1990 on when the bonds are cashed in to pay college tuition years later. The tax-free benefit is limited, though, to families with adjusted gross income less than $90,000 in the year the bonds are used to pay tuition. (For single or head-of-household taxpayers, the adjusted gross income limit for tax-free treatment of bonds used for tuition is $55,000.)

What Savings Bonds Are

U.S. savings bonds, like Treasuries, have the full faith and credit of the U.S. government backing them. But they are designed for individual savers and so are issued in smaller denominations and don't trade on the financial exchanges. The face value on Series EE bonds can be $50, $75, $100, $500, $1,000, $5,000, or $10,000. You pay *half* the face value when you buy the bond. Interest then accumulates at a rate that is 85% of the average yield on marketable Treasury securities with five-year maturities *or* 6% a year—whichever is *higher.* The interest rate is calculated every six months and becomes effective May 1 and November 1. If the average rate on five-year Treasuries in the previous six months is 8.5%, for instance, the rate on savings bonds for the next six months will be 7.2%. In order to receive that rate (or the minimum 6% guarantee), investors must hold the bonds for at least five years.

Buying the bonds is simple. Your bank can usually provide an application (PD 4882). The bank can generally issue the savings bond or you can send the application, together with a check, to the Federal Reserve Bank in your area (see Appendix A) or to the Bureau of Public Debt, Parkersburg, WV 26106-1328. You can find out what the current rate on savings bonds is by calling, toll-free: 1-800-US-BONDS.

What You Must Know Before Making a Choice

Since the investment earnings of a child under 14 years of age can be taxable at the parents' tax rate, the standard use of savings bonds has been to buy the bonds in the child's UGMA or UTMA custodial account to mature when he or she is age 14 or older. Then the federal income tax would be at the child's presumably lower rate. Making that part of your strategy for building a college fund still makes sense, provided you are willing to put the assets irrevocably in the name of your child.

For some families, starting in 1990, the use of these bonds is now broader. They will be an attractive investment alternative because they will be the only investments with the full faith and credit of the U.S. behind them that will pay tax-free interest to parents who qualify. The trouble is, at the time you buy the bonds, you cannot be entirely sure they will deliver tax-free benefits to your family when they are cashed in years later.

The year the savings bonds are cashed in and used for tuition, some federal income tax will be due on those who file a joint federal tax return with adjusted gross income of $60,000 or more. (Married taxpayers must file a joint return to qualify for any tax benefits in using the bonds for tuition.) Those with adjusted gross incomes of

$90,000 or more in those years will get no federal tax benefit at all. For single and head-of-household taxpayers, the tax benefit starts to diminish at $40,000 and ends entirely at $55,000. (These figures will be adjusted upward for inflation if necessary.)

Parents cannot evade these income limitations by putting the savings bonds in the names of their children or other individuals. The law specifically states that the tax benefit is available only to bonds bought from January 1, 1990, on, by individuals then 24 years or older, and is "not allowable if bonds are purchased by a parent and put in the name of the child or another dependent of the taxpayer."

If the amount of savings bonds redeemed in a year—principal plus interest—is *more* than tuition and fees, the amount of tax-free interest is reduced in proportion. For instance, if you redeem $20,000 in bonds in a year ($10,000 of which is principal and $10,000 of which is income) and the tuition and fees for the year amount to only $15,000, the ratio of expenses to redemption value is 75%. So, $7,500 of the interest can be excluded from income for tax purposes, if the family meets the income limitations. The other $2,500 is fully taxable by the IRS. Tax-free income from the bonds, therefore, cannot be used to cover other college expenses such as books, transportation, and living costs.

Obviously, you will not know with certainty what your income will be the year you cash in the bonds to pay for a child's tuition, so you cannot be entirely sure of the tax benefit you'll receive. Furthermore, if your child delays entry into college so that you do not have to pay tuition in the year the savings bond matures, the income will be taxable to you if you cash in the bond. You may not want to hold the bond beyond that time, unless the Treasury makes some specific rules to cover this problem, because, at present, not all savings bonds pay interest beyond their maturity date. Of course, if your child does not go to college, or goes to one with a relatively low tuition, you may wind up paying federal tax anyway on all or some of the value of bonds you cash in.

If the income from savings bonds *might* be tax-free for your family, you should then consider how the interest rate available on the bonds stacks up against alternative taxable investments. The table on the next page summarizes the trade-off for three tax brackets—15%, 28%, and 33%.

Caution: At the 33% tax bracket, family incomes are likely to be running up into the range where income on the bonds will *not* be fully tax-free—and may be fully taxable at the federal level. For those parents, the equivalent yield that would make taxable investments a good alternative would be *lower* than the amount shown on the table. Using a lower figure in general in comparing alternative investments is probably wise, given the unusual uncertainty a saver faces about whether savings-bond income will or will not be taxed in the future when used for tuition.

YIELDS NEEDED ON TAXABLE INVESTMENTS TO EQUAL TAX-FREE YIELDS ON U.S. SAVINGS BONDS USED TO PAY TUITION AND FEES

INTEREST ON SAVINGS BONDS TO BE USED TO PAY TUITION (%)	% EQUIVALENT YIELD REQUIRED FROM TAXABLE INVESTMENTS AT		
	15% BRACKET	28% BRACKET	33% BRACKET
4.5	5.29	6.25	6.72
5.0	5.88	6.94	7.46
5.5	6.48	7.64	8.21
6.0	7.06	8.33	8.96
6.5	7.65	9.03	9.70
7.0	8.24	9.72	10.45
7.5	8.82	10.42	11.19
8.0	9.41	11.11	11.94
8.5	10.00	11.81	12.69
9.0	10.59	12.50	13.43
9.5	11.18	13.19	14.18
10.0	11.77	13.89	14.93

Appropriateness Guide

Early Planners whose adjusted gross income is not likely to go above $60,000 by the time they cash their savings bonds to pay tuition should consider them an easy, safe way to contribute to a college fund.

Some college-fund builders in this category might be tempted to think about borrowing against equity in a house (producing interest deductions) and using the proceeds to buy savings bonds that can accumulate interest tax-free. The tax law, however, prohibits the deduction of interest on these loans to purchase tax-free securities.

Late Starters who have at least five years until they must cash in their savings bonds to pay tuition expenses could find them an effective college-fund investment, especially if they anticipate that their income will not go up enough to reduce the federal tax benefits. Because the time horizon for this group of parents is shorter, they may be less uncertain about their future income (and, thus, the savings bonds' tax-free benefits). This means they can make a sounder decision about the bonds' value.

Last-minute Savers might be able to make some use of the Savings Bonds to pay tuition during the last years of college. The bonds must be held for at least five years to generate their maximum return.

12

Insurance: When It's Useful for Your College Fund

Universal life insurance policies can serve a dual purpose for college fund investors: They provide the parents of dependent children with the security of insurance *and* a way to build up assets by disciplined savings. Furthermore, a wisely purchased policy can provide fairly priced *lifetime* insurance coverage for the parents, adapt to their needs as they advance in age, and accumulate value to tap for retirement income later in life.

Not much more than twenty years ago there were only two types of widely available life insurance:

- *Term,* which insures a person for a specified period of time, usually one, five, ten or twenty years and pays a benefit only if the person dies during that period. It has no cash value. The premium you pay for this so-called *pure insurance* increases with the age of the insured individual.
- *Whole life* (often called *permanent* or *straight* life), in which the premium, the death benefit and the cash value are guaranteed for the life of the contract. *Participating* whole life policies make up the bulk of whole life policies now sold. In participating policies, dividends are generally paid annually. After you've owned such a policy for a number of years, these dividends can be a substantial offset to premiums or add to the death benefit.

The cash value of an insurance policy is its investment component. There's no mystery about how cash value is generated. The premium paid by the insurance buyer for any policy that offers cash value is applied, by the insurance company, to three areas: (1) a mortality charge to fund the pure insurance, based on the insured person's age, sex, and health; (2) commissions and administrative fees; with the remainder going into (3) an investment account, which builds cash value for the policy owner.

By tradition, insurance companies have been fairly conservative investors. That was certainly the case when a good share of their business was in a fixed cash value product—whole life. When interest rates began to increase sharply, however, during the late 1960s and 1970s, insurance customers turned away from the low yields on those policies. Or, they borrowed against the accumulated cash value at the very low interest charges they were entitled to in their policies and invested the cash elsewhere. As money-market funds, high-interest CDs and other investment products became readily available to individuals, the majority of insurance buyers opted for lower-cost term insurance. If they were disciplined savers, they then invested the savings on their premiums directly with brokerage firms, funds, or in CDs.

In response, insurance companies developed policies in which cash value builds up at rates comparable to that of other conservative investment alternatives. One of the most successful of these new policies is universal life, which is flexible, easy to understand and cost effective when purchased intelligently.

What Universal Life Insurance Is

Before you commit yourself to a universal life insurance contract, you'll be given a projection that will generally show you year by year how the death benefit and the cash value will change under both the guaranteed rate and the current rate of interest. You'll also be told what the guaranteed interest rate is on your policy (the lowest rate the company can pay on the investment portion) and the current rate of interest the company is actually paying.

The special feature of most universal life policies is that they are flexible. You can generally suspend premium payments for a time or increase the premiums to build up cash value more quickly, borrow against cash value or make partial withdrawals. They can adapt to the differing insurance needs you may experience at various stages in your life, including the period when you are building up a college fund.

Like most life insurance, universal life enjoys special status under current tax laws. Death benefits are *not* taxed to the recipients. And the cash value increases on a tax-deferred basis, which means that earned interest is not currently taxed. Under current tax laws, if you borrow against the cash value, you do not pay tax on the sum withdrawn. If you surrender the policy or make partial withdrawals of the cash value, however, you are liable for current tax on the amount you receive *less* the sum of premiums you've paid.

What You Must Know Before Making a Choice

A universal life policy can be an effective addition to your college fund *if you need the insurance.* So your first step is to assess that need. And the best time to do that is at your leisure, taking your time—not in the presence of a salesperson. A simple way to identify an insurance gap:

1. Estimate the annual expense of maintaining your household's current standard of living.

2. Estimate your household income following the death of a major provider.

3. Estimate the income that could reasonably be generated by investing the lump sums payable to family survivors from pension and profit-sharing plans and existing life insurance policies.

4. If there is a gap between estimated expenses and income, *you might consider adding additional life insurance as part of your college fund plan.* To get a clearer idea of the scope of your need, in the future use the Rule of 72 (page 106) to make a rough estimate of how the income and expense totals might look around the time your child is ready for college. For instance, an annual inflation rate of 5% would double the current annual expense and income figures in just over 14 years ($72 \div 5 = 14.4$), or around the year 2004. At a 6% inflation rate, the figures could double in 12 years ($72 \div 6 = 12$), around the year 2001.

If you've sent in the coupon on page 192 for your PaineWebber College Savings Plans, one of the four savings plans you receive will show you the lump sum you'll need at the start of your child's college years to pay for the college you've selected. You can use that figure, too, to assess the size of the death benefit needed merely to meet this anticipated expense if a family provider dies.

WORKSHEET: SHOULD INSURANCE BE PART OF YOUR COLLEGE FUND?

1. ANNUAL EXPENSES

Housing		
Rent	______	
Mortgage	______	
Utilities	______	
Property, water taxes	______	
Food		
Home	______	
Away from home	______	
Clothing/upkeep	______	
Transportation	______	
Education	______	
Private instruction	______	
Savings toward college fund	______	
Entertainment	______	
Recreation and vacation	______	
Medical and dental bills	______	
Insurance premiums		
Auto	______	
Disability	______	
Health	______	
Life	______	
Other	______	
Loan payments (except mortgage)	______	
Taxes		
Local (except property)	______	
State	______	
Federal	______	
TOTAL ANNUAL EXPENSES		______

2. SURVIVORS' ANNUAL INCOME

Surviving spouse's salary	________
Investment income	
Interest and dividends	________
Annuity or trust	________
Real estate rentals	________
Social Security/Veterans' benefits	________
TOTAL SURVIVORS' ANNUAL INCOME BEFORE PROCEEDS FROM LUMP-SUM DEATH BENEFITS	________

3. LUMP-SUM DEATH BENEFITS AVAILABLE TO INVEST

Pension or profit-sharing		
$ ________ invested @ 8% =	________	
Life insurance		
$ ________ invested @ 8% =	________	
INCOME AVAILABLE FROM INVESTMENT OF DEATH BENEFITS		________
4. INSURANCE GAP: Survivor Income + Income Available from Investment of Death Benefits — Household Expenses		________

How to Buy Insurance Wisely

Next you'll have to decide whether to fill an insurance gap by buying term insurance or universal life. If the gap between your household's expenses and its income after the loss of a major provider is substantial, especially during your child's college years, a five-year term policy to cover the extraordinary expenses during that period could be the most economical choice.

On the other hand, *Early Planners* who incorporate a universal life policy as one of the components of their college fund could be protected by a substantial death benefit, use the cash value build-up to help meet college expenses, and then continue the policy to build financial resources for retirement and to provide a financial legacy.

The policies also are an easy way for *grandparents* to help their children and grandchildren while remaining in control of the build-up of cash value, which they might need to meet personal financial emergencies during their own lifetimes. The parents of a 35-year-old male parent, for instance, might insure the life of their son with a PaineWebber Provider universal life insurance policy upon the birth of their first grandchild. The grandparents would contribute the $2,000 premium each year and be the owners of the policy. As owners they could borrow against the cash value or even surrender the policy. Their son would be named contingent owner, which means that the policy would continue in force with the son as owner when the parents died.

The "ledger sheet projection" of just such a PaineWebber *Provider* policy (page 136) is the sort of information you would get if you considered such a purchase. The insured individual is a 35-year-old male nonsmoker. In this example, year-by-year projections of death benefits and cash values are shown both for the 4% interest guaranteed by the Provider contract and for an 8% interest rate. (In mid-1989, Provider was actually paying 9%.)

The initial death benefit in this example is $157,000. It would continue to go up with each yearly $2,000 premium payment. After the 17th year of the policy's life, when the grandchild would be ready to begin college, $34,000 in premiums would have been paid, the son's family would be protected by a death benefit of $220,162 and the cash value of the policy would be $63,162.

At that point, the grandparents might have died, leaving the insured parent as the owner of the policy, responsible for the $2,000 annual premium.

With college expenses making a sizable dent in the family's budget, the father in this example chooses to suspend premium payments for four years while the family pays tuition bills. During those four years, he borrows $12,000 a year (not taxable under current tax laws) against the cash value of the policy to contribute toward his child's college expenses. (In four years, the loans reduce the death benefit of the policy by $38,000.)

The net cost of this loan, in a Provider contract at present, is zero for any amount up to 10% of the *account value.* The account value is listed in the ledger projection on page 136 and would be $62,162 in this example, where the policy earned 8% a year for 17 years. The account value and cash value of the policy would be the same. (During

PAINEWEBBER *PROVIDER* UNIVERSAL LIFE POLICY

Ledger prepared for 35-year-old male, preferred risk

First year annualized premium:	**$2,000**
Initial death benefit:	**Specified amount ($157,000) plus cash value**
Guaranteed interest rate:	**4%**
Assumed current rate:	**8%**

				4% guaranteed			8% current		
END OF YR.	AGE	ANNUAL-IZED PAYMT.	ANNUAL LOANS	DEATH BENEFIT	ACC'T. VALUE	CASH VALUE	DEATH BENEFIT	ACC'T. VALUE	CASH VALUE
1	35	2,000	0	158,885	1,885	0	158,885	1,885	0
2	36	2,000	0	160,707	3,707	1,401	160,904	3,904	1,432
3	37	2,000	0	162,582	5,582	3,276	163,083	6,083	3,519
4	38	2,000	0	164,511	7,511	5,205	165,418	8,418	5,754
5	39	2,000	0	166,496	9,496	7,190	187,920	10,920	8,150
TOTAL		10,000							
6	40	2,000	0	168,532	11,532	9,348	170,666	13,666	10,901
7	41	2,000	0	170,621	13,621	11,573	173,612	16,612	13,857
8	42	2,000	0	172,764	15,764	13,960	176,774	19,774	17,129
9	43	2,000	0	174,958	17,958	16,398	180,164	23,164	21,404
10	44	2,000	0	177,204	20,204	19,051	183,806	26,806	25,653
TOTAL		20,000							
11	45	2,000	0	179,510	22,510	21,737	187,728	30,728	29,955
12	46	2,000	0	181,875	24,875	24,495	191,949	34,949	34,563
13	47	2,000	0	184,299	27,299	27,299	196,492	39,492	39,492
14	48	2,000	0	186,780	29,780	29,780	201,405	44,405	44,405
15	49	2,000	0	189,315	32,315	32,315	206,699	49,699	49,699
TOTAL		30,000							
16	50	2,000	0	192,178	35,178	35,178	213,165	56,165	56,165
17	51	2,000	0	195,108	38,108	38,108	220,162	63,162	63,162
18	52	0	12,000	183,179	26,179	26,179	212,353	55,353	55,353
19	53	0	12,000	170,154	13,154	13,154	203,621	46,621	46,621
20	54	0	12,000	*	*	*	193,878	36,878	36,878
TOTAL			34,000	36,000					
21	55	0	12,000				182,607	25,607	25,607
22	56	4,370	0				188,056	31,056	31,056
23	57	4,370	0				193,887	36,887	36,887
24	58	4,370	0				200,113	43,113	43,113
25	59	4,370	0				206,766	49,766	49,766
TOTAL		51,480	48,000						

END OF YR.	AGE	ANNUAL-IZED PAYMT.	ANNUAL LOANS	DEATH BENEFIT	ACC'T. VALUE	CASH VALUE	DEATH BENEFIT	ACC'T. VALUE	CASH VALUE
26	60	4370	0				213,865	56,865	56,865
27	61	4,370	0				221,427	64,427	64,427
28	62	4,370	0				229,496	72,496	72,496
29	63	4,370	0				238,053	81,053	81,053
30	64	4,370	0				233,768	90,285	90,285
TOTAL		73,330	48,000						
50	84	0	3,500				169,082	144,290	144,290

*Further premium payments would be required in order to keep the contract in force on the guaranteed basis.

the first 12 years of the policy, there is a surrender charge if the policy owner cancels the policy. After that, these surrender charges vary from policy to policy.) In our example this parent is borrowing *over* 10% of the policy's account value and, under the current PaineWebber Provider contract would pay net interest of 2% a year on the portion of the loan over the no-cost limit. That annual interest cost is reflected in subsequent cash values of his policy.

Once college expenses are over, this parent may continue the $2,000 annual premium, but instead elects to increase annual premium payments to the maximum of $4,370 a year in order to build up cash value for retirement. After the 30th year of the contract, when the parent would be 65 years old, he stops paying premiums into the *Provider.*

Then he begins to take tax-free income of $3,500 a year through policy loans against the cash value. (If his tax bracket were low, he might instead have chosen to take income through withdrawals and pay taxes on it.)

By the time this policy holder reaches the age of 85, the death benefit still amounts to over $169,000—a tax-free legacy for his family. The difference, though, at this point between the death benefit and the policy's cash value ($144,290) is only $24,792, which is actually all the "insurance" left to the contract. At some point before, this policy holder could have decided to withdraw his remaining cash value, pay the income tax (on the difference between cash value and premiums paid to that point), and either use the cash for living expenses or reinvest it.

For the thirty years that premiums were paid in this example, the policy owners' cash outlay was $73,330. Based on the projected 8% annual interest rate, if the policy owner had surrendered it at that point, the annual rate of return on the policy would have been 6.17% before tax—*plus* the value of insurance coverage during those 30 years. If he died at 65, however, the death benefit of $233,768 would have meant an annual return of 10.09%—*tax free to his beneficiaries.* If he had died ten or twenty years earlier, the return to the family would have been substantially higher.

This comparison makes two things clear: (1) You pay something for the value of the insurance if you select a universal life policy as a component of your college fund; (2) the policy makes economic sense if insurance is important to you.

The value of the insurance to you and your family, therefore, should be your prime concern in deciding whether to incorporate a universal life policy in your college fund planning. The fact that interest earnings on your policy accumulate on a tax-deferred basis or the appealing feature of borrowing against your collateral in the insurance policy at a modest interest charge can be attractive, of course.

A universal life insurance policy offers a guaranteed interest rate, but also shows projections using a current interest rate. This current rate generally tracks current economic conditions and may vary up *or* down. In an effort to measure certain levels of your downside risk, you may want to have an illustration run using rates less than the current rate.

Don't assume, either, that the policy offering the highest current interest is the best buy. Policies differ significantly in their expenses and in their mortality charges. (In a survey of 171 universal life contracts in January 1989, *Best's Review* found the average monthly mortality charge for a 45-year-old nonsmoking male to be $0.22 per $1,000 of insurance, with some companies charging nearly $0.60 per $1,000 and others $0.06 per $1,000.) Furthermore, if the policy offers an unusually high current rate, take a close look at the company behind it.

Certainly make sure that you don't buy from an insurance company rated below A by A.M. Best, which measures insurance companies' financial strength. Your broker will give you the rating or you can check for yourself by looking up the company in the A.M. Best rating book found in most major libraries.

When purchasing a universal life contract, you should consider a long-term commitment of premium payments. Surrendering contracts early could return you less than your out-of-pocket cost in spite of the fact you had insurance coverage during these early years.

Appropriateness Guide

Universal life insurance policies are appropriate for *Early Planners* who value the insurance. Many policy owners need at least 10 years to build up enough cash value to make the substantial borrowing for college expenses practical. The policies can continue to be a wealth-building tool for individuals who want continuing insurance coverage and an opportunity to accumulate cash value for retirement later in life.

Term insurance is appropriate for *Early Planners, Late Starters* and *Last-minute Savers* who value the security of insurance coverage for their child's college expenses in the event of the untimely death of one of the family's providers.

13

Tax-Free Municipals: Making Sure They're for You

As soon as the federal government trimmed opportunities to cut taxes by shifting income to children, municipal bonds became far more attractive to parents as a college-fund building block. Even though federal tax rates are now lower than they have been for years, the appeal of not paying taxes on income is so great that many individuals continue to invest in municipals even when their anticipated return on the bonds is about the same, or only a trace higher than they could earn—after paying taxes—on alternative investments. One important consideration tipping the scale in favor of municipals for many long-term investors, of course, has been their concern that federal tax rates will eventually be raised to bring down the deficit. Clearly, establishing that a municipal-bond investment is tax-free is only the first step in making a sound decision to add them to your college fund.

What Municipals Are

Municipal bonds are the debt securities issued by state and local governments or by local authorities considered to be municipal entities under state laws. While municipal bonds are issued for a variety of purposes, state and local governments generally issue debt to raise capital necessary to finance infrastructure projects. Local authorities, on the other hand, issue bonds to provide capital for non-profit governmental services such as public power, waste management, utilities (water and sewer), and hospitals.

Municipal governments are granted the right under federal tax laws to sell their securities free of federal income tax on interest paid to the investor. In most cases, state and local laws allow tax exemptions on an investor's interest earnings on municipal debt securities issued within the specific state. Municipal interest earnings on certain investments, therefore, are tax-free at the state and local level as well as the federal level.

The broadest type of municipals are general-obligation bonds (GOs), backed by the full faith and credit of the state or city government, which means that the bonds are secured by the taxing power of the entity that issues them. Because of the full-faith and credit pledge, these bonds are generally considered the most secure. But their ratings do vary. Since local governments generally rely heavily on property and income taxes for revenues, bonds issued by communities with rising real-estate values, good demographic trends, a positive image with industry, and a history of being able to raise appropriate taxes get the best ratings.

Revenue bonds are the other chief category of municipals. Principal and interest on these bonds is paid back to bondholders from revenues generated by a specific project, such as the operation of a road, bridge, public utility, or water-treatment plant. Historically, investors consider GOs to be higher-quality municipals than revenue bonds, but you could make a mistake investing on that premise without looking more closely at the issue you have under consideration. A number of revenue bonds actually have higher ratings than some GOs.

What You Must Know Before Making a Choice

As a first step, check the expected yield on any tax-free municipal investment you have under consideration. Use the table on page 142 to compare the expected municipal yield against the equivalent yield for a fully taxed investment. This will be the yield you would need to earn on the taxable security to equal a tax-free return on the municipal.

Some states tax the interest earned by their citizens on bonds issued by *other* states. And if you're unlucky enough to live in a city that levies an income tax, you may have to ask a broker for municipals that qualify as "triple-tax free." If you choose to put a good share of your college fund into municipals, however, diversify your holdings among a variety of issuers. And if you live in a state where you *can* buy out-of-state bonds and avoid state taxes on the income, do consider taking advantage of the opportunity to diversify geographically.

YIELDS REQUIRED ON TAXABLE INVESTMENTS TO EQUAL TAX-FREE YIELDS (1988 TAX RATES)

AT THIS TAXABLE INCOME		FEDERAL	A TAX-FREE YIELD OF				
HEAD OF HOUSEHOLD	JOINT RETURN	TAX BRACKET	6%	7%	8%	9%	10%
(in thousands)			EQUALS A TAXABLE YIELD OF:				
$0–23.9	$0–29.8	15%	7.1%	8.2%	9.4%	10.6%	11.8%
23.9–61.7	29.8–71.9	28%	8.3	9.7	11.1	12.5	13.9
61.7–123.8	71.9–149.3	33%	9.0	10.5	11.9	13.4	14.9
Over 123.8	Over 149.3	28%	8.3	9.7	11.1	12.5	13.9

Obviously, it takes a great deal of special expertise to evaluate whether the stream of revenues pledged to the payment of municipal securities is sufficient to meet obligations in a timely manner. Adding to the complexity, no central authority, such as the Securities and Exchange Commission, sets standards for what must be disclosed by issuers. The states and municipalities raising the money provide information voluntarily, though they have to respond to any demands for clarification made by the securities dealers who sell the issues to investors. The SEC and the securities industry are now working together on disclosure guidelines for municipal issues.

Municipals are, nevertheless, generally accepted to be second only to U.S. government securities in risk. The municipal default rate overall has been less than 1% since the depression of the 1930s—but defaults *do* occur. Assessing the likelihood that any problem will arise in the prompt payment of interest is the job of the major bond-rating agencies, Moody's Investor Service and Standard & Poor's. On bonds which are rated by these agencies, a municipal entity's ability to pay is assessed at the time of issuance, with updates provided throughout the life of the bonds as deemed necessary by the rating agencies. Although a rating agency assessment will include numerous in-depth reviews, generally the agency will determine an entity's ability to pay principal and interest in a timely manner. Revenue-raising powers and willingness to pay, which is reflected in the political climate that usually surrounds tax-rate increases, are included in the evaluation. Leading securities firms don't rely entirely on Moody's and Standard & Poor's ratings. Employing their own municipal bond research staffs, assessments of the credit quality of bonds offered for sale are made independently of the rating agencies.

Since there are hundreds of thousands of municipal issues on the market, not all of them *are* rated. Limit the choices for your college fund, though, to those that are rated. And if you choose to buy municipals directly, you'll probably be buying only a few issues, so for safety's sake narrow your sights still further to those that are at least investment-grade. The table on the next page defines the investment-grade categories.

There's yet another way to limit your risk on a municipal bond: Buy an insured bond. In the event an issuer fails to meet its obligations in a timely manner, principal and interest is guaranteed by a noncancelable contract with a municipal bond insurance company. These specialized companies strive to maintain top credit ratings. So, when they insure a bond from a community that might have earned only a BBB rating on its own, the bond is AAA-rated. That means, however, the bond will generally yield less than an uninsured BBB issue.

Insured bonds are especially attractive for college-fund investments. The added safety factors are probably worth the modest loss of yield. Remember, insurance applies only to the payment of interest and principal. It will not protect you against market risk—decrease in the value of a municipal if interest rates go up. The investor must be comfortable with owning the underlying credit quality.

How to Buy Municipals and Municipal-Bond Funds Wisely

Investors can purchase municipal bonds directly from their brokerage firms or can buy shares in a municipal-bond fund. Generally purchasing municipals directly allows the investor the flexibility of managing his or her own portfolio. If you are buying bonds for a college fund, for instance, you will not only be able to specify credit quality but also the exact maturity matching the years when you'll need the bond proceeds to pay tuition. As an individual buying and selling a few

WHAT MUNICIPAL-BOND RATINGS MEAN

MOODY'S		STANDARD & POOR'S	
Aaa	The best quality. They carry the smallest degree or risk and are generally referred to as "gilt-edge." Interest payments are protected by a large or by an exceptionally stable margin and principal is secure.	AAA	Capacity to pay interest and repay principal is extremely strong.
Aa	High quality by all standards. Rated lower than the best bonds because margins of protection may not be as large as Aaa securities or fluctuation of protective elements may be . . . greater or there may be other elements present which make the long-term risks appear somewhat larger than Aaa securities.	AA	Very strong capacity to pay interest and repay principal. Differs from the highest-rated issues only by a small degree.
A	Upper-medium-grade securities. Factors giving security to principal and interest are considered adequate, but elements may be present which suggest a susceptibility to impairment some time in the future.	A	Strong capacity to pay interest and repay principal, although it is somewhat more susceptible to the adverse effects of changes in circumstances and economic conditions than debt in higher-rated categories.
Baa	Medium-grade obligations, neither highly protected nor poorly secured. Certain protective elements may be lacking or may be characteristically unreliable over any great length of time.	BBB	Adequate capacity to pay interest and repay principal. Adverse economic conditions or changing circumstances are more likely to lead to a weakened capacity to pay interest and repay principal than in higher-rated categories.

municipal bonds (the minimum lot is generally $5,000, which is five bonds), you are at a disadvantage doing much trading in municipals, even though it is a very liquid market. Individuals now buy most of the municipals issued (including investors in municipal-bond funds and unit investment trusts) but the bulk of the bond trading is done in multimillion-dollar lots between big institutions. Prices are set by broker-to-broker trading all across the nation in what is, in essence, an over-the-counter market.

The difference (called the "spread") between Treasuries and highly rated municipals of the same maturity is one important fact to keep your eye on to figure out when municipals appear to be a particularly good bargain.

Yields on municipals generally hover *below* the yields on Treasuries for one basic reason: As an investor, you have to pay federal income tax on Treasuries but not on municipals. Even if you buy a municipal from another state and have to pay tax on the bond's interest income, the cost will probably be far lower than the federal income-tax rate.

Municipal-Bond Funds and Unit Investment Trusts

Buying municipals in a mutual fund or unit investment trust rather than directly solves two problems for many investors:

1. Their minimum purchase is generally much lower than buying a $25,000 lot of municipals, or even a $5,000 odd lot.

2. Funds and UITs offer small investors portfolio diversification they could not achieve themselves without investing much larger sums of money.

You might earn somewhat less in a fund of municipal-bond issues than in a wisely selected group of bonds you own directly, but that is by no means certain. True, funds subtract administrative costs from fund revenues and, in some cases, sales commissions or exit fees. On the other hand, fund managers are able to bargain more effectively on price because of their high volume of trading.

If you select a municipal mutual fund, you may also profit from astute timing decisions made by managers of the fund, who are generally attempting to produce trading profits as well as interest income. These capital gains (if the trading is successful) together with interest generated by the municipal bonds makes up *total return.* Trading yourself, with the municipals in your college fund, however, can be risky and costly.

You'll probably get several streams of income from a municipal-bond mutual fund, but only the portion attributable to *exempt interest income* earned by the bonds in the fund's portfolio is free of federal taxes. At the end of the year, the fund will give you a statement of the tax status of whatever it paid out to you. *Profits made by trading bonds are taxable to bond shareholders as capital gains when they're paid out to fund shareholders.* (You also owe tax if you sell an individual municipal bond for more than you paid for it.)

For investors who select a municipal-bond mutual fund with a satisfactory performance record, another advantage is the ease with which earnings can be reinvested right back into the fund. That convenience can also be a trap. Remember, you should continue to appraise alternatives as your college-fund assets build up, tax rates change, interest rates move up and down, and your children grow closer and closer to college age. At some point, for instance, it might be better to route your municipal-bond income into Treasuries, other government issues, or even bank CDs.

College-fund investors may also wish to consider municipal-bond unit investment trusts. Unlike mutual funds, these are fixed portfolios of bond obligations chosen by investment professionals to achieve current income rather than trading profits. Generally, as long as the bonds in the trust portfolio retain their sound investment quality they are held to maturity. (Should their quality be impaired by events as time goes on, they might be sold by the trustee bank before maturity date.) As long as the portfolio remains intact, the trust pays a relatively steady stream of income. As bonds mature, are called by their issuers or sold, the available principal is returned to unitholders.

UIT's are often specifically tailored. Some are insured for a higher degree of safety, while others may be state specific and will generate double tax-free income. Typical maturities of these trusts tend to be in the range of five, ten, or fifteen years. Your broker can arrange to have the income from the UIT flow directly to you for reinvestment, or into a tax-free money market account, or even into a managed municipal-bond fund. Just as you would when buying a municipal bond directly, remember to compare the UIT tax-free yield against what's available in taxable investments.

Inspect the UIT's portfolio of bonds, too, to make sure they're appropriate. Be wary of a trust portfolio that contains bonds with high-coupon rates relative to the current market. The stated rate of return on such a trust may look very enticing, but you may be paying a premium for the trust's units. If the issuers of the high-coupon bonds in the portfolio retire them early, you could suffer a capital loss . . . not to mention a significant reduction in your stated rate of return. Setting up the trust costs something, which you'll pay for in commissions and some expenses.

You can also buy a portfolio of fifty to seventy municipal bonds in a closed-end bond fund, although you probably ought to have a taste for more active investment than is necessary with a mutual fund or unit trust to maximize your return on this form of investment (as explained on page 100).

Appropriateness Guide

Early Planners: Insured municipals, municipal zeros, municipal UITs, and other municipal-bond funds are excellent base builders, so long as the after-tax yield is sufficient compared to what is available on taxable issues. Finding non-callable bonds with long maturities may be difficult, so be cautious about paying a premium for a bond.

Late Starters: Select bonds or unit trusts whose issuers have shorter maturities so you will have the cash available when tuition bills start. Bond mutual funds and closed-end funds are less appropriate, because the shorter time span increases the risk that you will have to redeem your shares during a down cycle in the bond market.

Last-minute Savers: Municipals that mature during the years you will be paying tuition bills are still appropriate for new savings especially during unusual market situations when the spread between yields on short-term municipals and yields on Treasury bills and money-market funds is very narrow.

14

Corporate Bonds: Income vs. Safety

Though safety was once a major selling point for corporate bonds, it's been many years since corporate bonds could be considered safer than common stocks except in the extreme case—bankruptcy. For many years now, the bond market—especially long-term bonds—has been swinging up and down with just about the same volatility as the stock market. More recently, with the wave of corporate takeovers and mergers, owners of many top-credit-rated corporate bonds suddenly found the value of their bonds skidding when the company's debt suddenly ballooned as it defended itself against a takeover or was taken private through a leveraged buyout. Paradoxically, at the same time that worries are surfacing about top-rated corporate debt, investors' appetite for low-credit-rated, high-yield (junk) corporate bonds surprises even many of the professionals in the securities business who sell them.

In this rapidly shifting investment environment, you have to proceed cautiously when investing part of your college fund in corporate debt.

What Corporate Bonds Are

Bonds are certificates of debt. In exchange for agreeing to accept a fixed rate of return, the bond investor usually gets only one guarantee: that he stands in line ahead of a company's owners, the common-stock and preferred stockholders, to collect from bankruptcy trustees if the company goes under. Owning a corporate bond doesn't guarantee that its stream of interest income will continue. Income can be assured only by the financial condition of the company and its prospects.

When a company has a relatively high level of debt in relation to the total value of its common shares, it is said to be *leveraged.* In a healthy company that is able to make more profit on its borrowed capital (its debt) than it pays out in interest, leverage can be a very successful technique to raise the value of its *common shares.* Since the amount of earnings that has to be paid out to bond owners is fixed, a higher proportion of earnings flows to the company's common shares, so the market value of the company's stock should rise. Obviously, leverage is of no value to the company's bondholders. Actually, the more debt on a company's books, the more its bondholders are at risk during a recession or an industry downturn because the cash the company needs to pay interest shrinks.

What You Must Know Before Making a Choice

Adding corporate bonds to your college fund as a safer alternative to common stock is a debatable decision. The yield to maturity you receive is a function of not only how much you paid for the bond initially but at what rate you reinvest interest payments. The bond's yield to maturity is based on the price you pay for it initially. (That assumes, of course, that you hold the bond until it matures rather than trade it in an attempt to achieve capital gains.) Bond investors don't have what common-stock investors have—the prospect of sharing in a company's increasing profits—although good performance might result in the bond being upgraded which could result in a capital gain if the bond is sold before maturity.

Your purpose in adding corporate bonds to your college investment fund is usually to lift your overall rate of return above what you could get by investing exclusively in Treasuries and municipals. Clearly, you don't want to do that at the risk of losing capital. No yield difference would be sufficient to cover that loss. The dean of conservative investing, Benjamin Graham, warned that bond investment is "a negative art, and the investor should never lose sight of that fact." In other words, when you consider putting corporate bonds into your college fund, it should not be with a view toward gains so much as assuring a stream of income and the safety of your principal. When you are assessing the reliability of the company that stands behind the bonds, you must pay more attention to its ability to withstand bad times than its ability to profit in good times.

So, take some of these key factors into account in evaluating bonds for investments:

• *The type of company and its size.* A company in a cyclical business (metals, mining, construction) needs a higher margin of safety than a company in a more stable industry (food, cosmetics, health supplies). One commonly used safety margin: The company's flow of cash per share is greater than what it must pay in interest per share. Ask your broker for this information or find it yourself in some company annual reports and many securities research reports. Cash flow per share is basically the company's net income and depreciation divided by its outstanding shares. Though big companies can certainly get into serious trouble, smaller enterprises, in general, are more vulnerable during severe downturns.

• *Provisions to protect the rights of bondholders.* These so-called covenants might include traditional positive features such as a sinking fund (the company is required to make regular cash payments into the fund to be be used to retire the bond issue), safeguards against issuing additional bonds, and requirements to meet certain financial ratios. These protections are more necessary than ever nowadays to protect investors in high-quality corporate bonds against the risk that their bonds will sink in value as a result of sudden new additions to debt.

• *Call provisions.* Nearly all corporate bonds (like many municipal bonds) have a provision that enables management to pay off the bond before maturity at a stipulated price. That price is usually a premium over the face value of the bond, and it declines as the maturity date nears. These bonds are almost always called when interest rates decline, destroying your plan to realize a particular rate of return on your bond until it matures. The worst trap: Paying a premium for a bond that is called soon thereafter. A call provision virtually prevents you from realizing any appreciation in the value of the bond if interest rates fall. Nevertheless, you still face the risk of your bond's sliding in value if rates go up.

• *The relation and trend of earnings to interest payments.* For safety, many securities analysts look for the company's after-tax earnings to be 2.5 to 4 times its total fixed interest charges—with higher ratios required of companies in the more cyclical industries. A second check: In a poor earnings year, did the company's after-tax earnings amount to at least *twice* its fixed interest costs? (This is called an *earnings test.*) Ask your broker what measure his firm believes is appropriate for any corporate bond you have under consideration.

• *The value of the company as a going concern over the amount of its debt.* While the earnings test, defined above, is a measure of the firm's ability to meet its *interest* payments, this yardstick is a rough measure of the safety of your *principal.* A conservative measure: The market value of the company's stock equity (number of shares times the market value of each of its shares) is at least 1¼ times the value of its total debt. Sometimes, security analysts familiar with the company may consider the company's stock to be undervalued. They may suggest using the liquidating (or "breakup") value of the company instead of the market value of its shares as a measure.

How to Invest Wisely in Corporate Bonds and Bond Funds

Never let the search for higher yield and faster buildup of your college fund blind you to the all-important safety factors in investing in corporate bonds. Higher yields always mean higher risk. (And low yields don't automatically mean little risk.) Don't simply move your finger down a list of available bonds, select one that appears to offer a generous rate of return, and ask: What do I give up in safety to get this yield? You don't want to give up *any* of the safety requirements you and your investment adviser or broker consider basic to preserving the capital in your college fund and realizing a reasonable rate of return over time. *Settle on the criteria first, and then select the bond.*

For Early Planners, one effective bond-buying strategy could be to select investment-grade corporate bonds selling at a deep discount to their face value because the interest rate on the bonds is well below current rates. (You don't want a bond selling at a deep discount simply because the company is in financial trouble.) There would be little call risk on such bonds, and when they mature at face value, you will also achieve a capital gain. You will generally need about ten to sixteen years to make this an effective strategy. Choose bonds that mature when you expect to need the cash to meet college expenses. You could hold the bonds in your own name or in a custodian account for your child because of the relatively low, taxable, semi-annual interest payments. If the bonds are in a custodian account for your child once he or she reaches 14 years of age, the income *and capital gain* would be taxed at the child's federal tax rate.

Deep-discount bonds are quite different from the high-yield bonds that highly leveraged companies issue to attract investors to their bonds. Generally referred to as junk bonds, high-yield bonds are rated B or BB, rather than investment-grade A, AA, AAA and BBB (in Standard & Poor's Bond Guide). The default rate on junk bonds appears to have been low, although there is now controversy about interpretation of the data. But these companies are certainly more vulnerable to any economic hardship.

With safety such a key concern in the selection of corporate bonds, bond funds could be the logical alternative for college-fund investors. Certainly, in the case of high-yield bonds, the fund's diversification at least reduces an investor's risk when a sudden turnaround in a firm's performance, unexpected competition, or a sharp economic downturn imperils its ability to continue paying interest.

The goal of most corporate-bond mutual funds is to produce income, but, unlike conservative individual bond investors who hold a bond until it matures, fund managers also trade bonds, hoping to achieve capital gains by buying and selling at the right time. Unless a bond-fund manager is extremely agile, astute, and lucky, a corporate-bond fund, like any bond or bond fund, is likely to suffer capital losses when interest rates climb, which will reduce total return to the investor. In a time of falling interest rates, good fund management should be able to produce capital gains in addition to interest income.

Appropriateness Guide

Early Planners: Deep-discount investment-grade corporate bonds are suitable if selected to mature when college expenses are anticipated. Corporate-bond funds and carefully selected individual high-grade bond issues (preferably those with provisions that enable you to get back your initial investment in the event of a takeover, merger, or buyout) are also suitable. High-yield bonds should be purchased only in a fund.

Early Planners who want to avoid the volatility of bond funds in their college funds, or those who are closer to the years when they will start to tap the fund, could select a group of corporate-bond unit investment trusts of varying maturities instead of either a mutual fund or direct bond investments. As a further safety factor, some UITs of utility bonds are now insured against loss of principal and guarantee the continuation of interest payments—an upgrade in quality that comes at some loss in yield.

To minimize risk, make sure the corporate bond, government bond, municipal bond, and other fixed-interest investments in your college fund give you an overall mix of maturities.

Late Starters: Carefully selected high-grade bonds that mature during the years when you will need the cash for tuition are suitable.

A relatively short-term unit investment trust of corporate bonds is also suitable, provided that you have other, more liquid fixed-interest holdings so that you can take advantage of any rise in interest rates.

Bond mutual funds are generally not a top choice for new savings, because market risk is high, given the short time you have before the fund shares must be cashed in.

Last-minute Savers: A three-year unit investment trust of bonds is suitable. So is a carefully selected, high-quality corporate bond that matures during the years you will need the cash for tuition. (Make sure that you are satisfied with the yield to maturity after paying any necessary commissions.)

15

Stocks and Stock Funds: Safe Search for Growth

The annual return on common stock investments over the past 63 years has averaged 10%—6.9% over the rate of inflation for that period. That return has been achieved despite the 90% decline in stock prices following the 1929 crash and the nearly 50% drop in stock values during 1973–74, according to Ibbotson Associates, Inc., of Chicago. The Dow Industrial Index ended up higher by year-end 1987 than 1986, despite the record 503-point plummet of the Index on October 19, 1987. And in the year that followed, the average return on stocks was 10%, including dividends. Few, if any, other investments can match that long-term record. Therefore, putting some savings into equities either directly or through funds, makes sense for most college-fund investors during the early, wealth-building years of a long-term savings plan.

What Common Stocks Are

The stocks of only a tiny portion of the hundreds of thousands of companies in the U.S. are bought and sold by the public. The two big data services on stocks, Moody's and Standard & Poor's, report sales, earnings, and other information regularly on about seven thousand of these publicly held companies. But shares of only about five thousand companies trade actively.

You'll probably want to focus on a far smaller universe of companies in selecting specific shares for your college fund—companies with a solid history of earnings and dividend growth and with a healthy share of the markets in which they do business. If you invest in an aggressive-growth fund, you might be an indirect owner of shares in a somewhat wider group.

In either case, your shares represent ownership of their fair portion of a company's assets and of whatever flows to the company's "bottom line" (net income). The value of your shares will be determined by these fundamentals and—equally important—by *how much others want to own those assets and earnings.* As the investment banker-economist John Maynard Keynes once explained, the stock market is a beauty contest in which the object is not to select the most beautiful contestant but the contestant who will be chosen most beautiful.

What You Must Know Before Making a Choice

Once you've decided that stocks deserve a role in building up your college fund, the three key guidelines to successful stock investing, according to PaineWebber experts, are:

- Develop a disciplined approach to selecting stocks. Understand the basic criteria you're using to make a choice. (See below: "A disciplined approach.")
- Do as little short-term trading as possible. And don't "fight the tape" by leaping into a declining market because you're sure it's about to turn right around. Leave those decisions to traders.
- Keep an eye on the proportion of stocks in your college fund in relation to returns available from alternative investments. (Investment professionals call this "asset allocation.")

A Disciplined Approach

There are as many currents affecting the stock market as there are wind and ocean currents affecting the weather. They include general economic and industry ups and downs, interest rates, currency flows, technological changes, government regulation, international events, competitive challenges, good and bad management, taste and fashion, and the law. There's no way for you to make stock selections based on taking even a few of those factors into account systematically. The stocks in your college fund have one function: to generate fairly reliable growth at a rate somewhat better than can be achieved by

Treasuries and other fixed-interest investments. You shouldn't be in search of a "killing." For the most part, you're going to look for companies that already have a good track record of success available at a fair price. If you have a taste for a bit more risk, you might consider putting some part of the college fund's assets into a growth fund. The savings you set aside for your child's future should never be invested in a "tip," or in an "idea" that you don't fully understand. Take the time to be methodical and make long-lasting decisions that you can live with.

When you're considering an individual stock suggested by your broker or that you've researched yourself, ask yourself what you expect from the issue: Reasonably steady growth? Good dividend income? A sharp rise in price over the next one or two years? Check those expectations against the company's actual performance.

Too many investors look only at a company's net income per share, and, perhaps, at the five- or ten-year record of such earnings in the annual report. That gives you an idea of whether the company's earnings are steady or erratic. But you can quickly find out a lot more by knowing what else to look for in the company's annual report.

• *Estimate the cushion the company has against hard times* by looking at its total debt load. On the balance sheet you'll find the figures for *long-term debt, short-term debt,* and *shareholders' equity.* Figure out what percentage of total debt is represented by short-term debt and whether that percentage is increasing from quarter to quarter or year to year. That trend could make the company vulnerable to higher interest rates. Add the *long-term debt* and *shareholders' equity* figures together (the total is long-term capital). Then divide long-term debt by long-term capital. If the result is 50% or less, the company probably has additional borrowing capacity, which could be essential to take it through a period of exceptionally fast growth—or an earnings falloff.

• *Spot an early warning sign that sales might be about to slow down.* Figure out the rate at which *inventories* (also on the balance sheet) are rising. Compare that rate to the rate at which *sales* (on the profit-and-loss statement) are rising. If inventories are going up faster than sales, the company may already be producing more goods than it can sell.

• *Make sure management has a firm hand on costs*—a matter of increased concern now that competition can come from anyplace in the world. Figure out the annual rate of increase in expenses (on the company's profit-and-loss statement). Compare that to the rate of increase in sales. Costs may be getting out of line if expenses are going up faster than sales, and that could spell trouble for a fast-growing company.

• *Get some sense of whether management is honest about facing and dealing with negative business conditions.* Don't ignore the chief executive's letter that usually leads off an annual report. Look at the latest letter and the one in the previous year's annual report. If optimistic projections were made earlier, have they been borne out by results since? If they weren't, does management explain what happened and offer information on what's being done about it? Be wary of a management that doesn't acknowledge any problems at all in the year's operations.

By looking for clues like this yourself, you'll find that you will get more valuc out of your relation with a broker. You'll ask better questions, clarify your own thinking, and make investments that closely match your needs and your tolerance for risk. Of course, doing this yourself can be time consuming. These clues and others are what professional analysts at top brokerage firms search for every day. When you deal with such a firm, you can ask your investment executive to provide research reports on companies that you might be interested in.

What's a Fair Price?

Knowing that a company appears to be sound and its prospects promising isn't enough to make a wise stock selection. The stock also has to be available at a price that offers you some reasonable assurance it will perform at least as well as the stock market as a whole—or, preferably, better.

The usual measure used to evaluate prices on stocks is by *price-earnings ratios* (usually known as the *p/e ratio*). If a company has earned a total of $2.00 per share over the past four quarters, for instance, and is currently selling at $20.00 per share, its price-earnings ratio is 10 (20.00 divided by 2.00 = 10). Relating the stock's current price to past earnings is called, more specifically, the price-*trailing*-earnings ratio. If an analyst estimates that the company will earn $2.90 over the next twelve months, its $20.00 current price represents a 6.9 p/e ratio—or, more specifically, a 6.9 price-*projected*-earnings ratio.

The price-earnings ratios (on trailing earnings) are reported for individual company stocks in most newspapers' daily financial tables. The p/e ratios are also calculated regularly for the basic stock-market indices—the Dow Jones Industrial Average and the Standard & Poor's 500 Index. So, it is relatively easy to see whether an individual stock is selling at about the market's average, below it, or above it. Generally, stocks of companies with fast-growing earnings (or with prospects of fast growth) sell at relatively high price-earnings ratios based on trailing earnings (known as a "premium to market").

While the average price-earnings ratio for the S&P 500 Index might be 12 or 14, for instance, a well-regarded computer company might be at 20 and a genetic engineering company at 30 or more. This is because each industry also has its own normal p/e ratio. The stocks of many companies in high-growth or high-tech industries, for instance, often have a higher p/e ratio than stocks in industries such as autos or textiles. The stock of a company in a very cyclical business, such as mining or metal-working, might also sell at a very high price-trailing-earnings ratio just at the point that its earnings are turning upward—because the earnings in its immediate *past* are so low. So, the p/e ratio of a stock isn't enough information to decide whether the price is right.

Earnings per share might be relatively low, for instance, but *cash flow per share* could be very high, which may make the company an attractive merger candidate. Cash flow is made up of earnings plus depreciation and amortization. High cash flow makes it easier to pay down the increased debt that accompanies many mergers or acquisitions.

After a downturn in the stock market, investors usually begin to look more carefully again at other traditional measures of price—including price-book value ratios and price-sales ratios.

The *book value per share* for a company is reported in its annual report and also in standard investor services such as the *Value Line Stock Guide* and *Standard & Poor's Investment Service.* The book value per share of a company is computed by adding up all assets (generally *excluding* intangible assets, such as goodwill, patents, copyrights, trademarks, etc.), subtracting all liabilities and stock issues ahead of the common stock (such as preferred stock) and dividing the sum by the number of outstanding shares in the company. If a company's book value per share is $20.00 and it currently trades in the market at $15.00, it is selling *below book value.* Some stocks sell at or below book value because investors have overlooked them or they're in industries that aren't currently in favor on Wall Street. Many of them, though, are down at that level because the companies have severe market or financial problems.

Below-book-value stocks often become acquisition targets, though, if certain factors make them attractive. Real estate bought years ago may still be carried on the books at original cost and be worth far more, which means the book value is understated. Or the company may be made up of several separate businesses that could be sold off for cash. This means the book value is less than the company's "breakup" value.

A stock might also be described as bargain-priced because it has a low *price-sales ratio.* This is the company's current stock price divided by its sales revenues per share. A stock selling at $20.00 that had $50.00 of revenue per share would have a price-sales ratio of .40 (20 divided by 50). This sales ratio is not regularly reported for standard stock indices such as the Dow Jones Industrials or the S&P 500, but analysts who use it would consider a stock selling at a ratio of .50 or less to be worth looking at. (If the company has a very high level of debt, however, the low ratio could be deceptive.) This ratio does have the advantage of being less susceptible to complex accounting changes that sometimes distort earnings—and, thus, earnings-per-share measures. It might also be used as a supplement to the earnings-per-share measure to compare the prices of shares of companies in the *same* industry.

The other most common measure of the fairness of a stock's price is its *dividend yield*—how much the company paid shareholders in dividends over the past year in relation to the current stock price. This is calculated by dividing the annual dividend (say $2.50) by the stock's price (say $60.00) to arrive at the dividend yield (4.16%). This is a less important measure, however, for growth companies, which typically pour earnings right back into the business rather than pay high dividends. The dividend yield is reported in the stock tables in *The Wall Street Journal* and major daily newspapers. If one of the strong appeals of a stock you have under consideration is a high dividend yield—say, 10% while most stocks are yielding 4% or so—make sure to ask your broker (or research yourself) whether the company's earnings are healthy enough to sustain paying dividends at that rate.

Riding Through a Downturn

Whatever price you pay for your stocks early in the buildup of your college fund, chances are you will run into a stock-market downturn that will erode profits. Bear markets tend to recur in about four- or five-year intervals. The one that started in 1981 brought down prices about 24%; the one in 1977 by nearly 27%; the one in 1974 by over 45%; and the one in 1969 by about 36%. Probably the worst thing you can do to your overall rate of return on your stock investments is to sell in a panic during such a downturn. If you follow the College-Fund Investment Selection Guides in Part Two of this book, you're very likely to have time for a stock-market recovery before you have to move your holdings into more liquid investments. (That is why the Guidelines suggest that you generally begin to phase out of stocks and stock funds as your child approaches college age.)

A conservative and easy way to limit your losses on stock investments is with *stop-loss orders.* At the time you buy a stock, for instance, you could decide that you will not tolerate a loss of more than 10% or 15%. You give your broker an order to sell the stock at that point—say, when a stock you bought at $50.00 a share drops below $45.00 a share. Or you can use a stop-loss order to preserve a gain on a stock. Suppose the stock you bought at $50.00 goes to $60.00 a share. You think it can go to $70.00 but are unwilling to take the risk of losing all of your $10.00 per share gain. You could enter a stop-loss order to sell at $55.00 per share.

Stop-loss orders aren't foolproof, though. If the market falls precipitously in a single day (as it did October 19, 1987), the rush of transactions may make it impossible to sell your stock at the stop-loss price and, in that case, you'll be sold out at a lower price. Setting the price too close to the stock's current price can be a mistake, too. Because of day-to-day fluctuations, or even inter-day fluctuations, your stock holding may be sold even though the issue bounces right back and continues its upward movement. So, if you use stop-loss orders, allow room for the price to move a bit.

Study after study has concluded that the most consistently safe way to ride out downturns is by dollar-cost averaging. This means that an investor who plans to have some part of his college fund in stocks for at least five years would commit a fixed sum of money to stock investment, perhaps a monthly sum, and stick with it through market highs and lows. This kind of steady investing program is more likely to be successful if the company stocks purchased are fairly well diversified. That makes it especially well suited for investing in stock funds. (For more details, see Chapter Eight.) During market downturns, the fixed sum of money would buy more shares. Another discipline, if you have selected a few companies as long-term holdings, is to reinvest dividends back in more company shares, preferably buying right from the company via a dividend-reinvestment plan, which saves you brokerage commissions. The problem with this strategy for most people is that you must be able to confront the emotional pressures that usually push individual investors out of stocks during a bear market.

Figuring Out How Well You're Doing

The simplest measure of appreciation on your college fund's stock portfolio is the total return annually—dividends plus price gains (less commissions). You might also want to consider how well your stocks are doing compared to the overall stock market's gains (or losses). To do either or both requires very simple record-keeping—one stock per page in a small notebook. On the day you make a stock or stock-fund purchase, mark down the price paid per share, the commission, *and* the index number reported for one or two of the basic market measures listed below. Add dividends when you receive the checks. You now have everything you need to figure out your total return (and compare it to other investments in your college fund). And you can also occasionally measure the relative performance of each of your stock holdings against the overall market.

The basic market averages, which are usually reported in the financial pages of your local newspaper and are always in *The Wall Street Journal* or, weekly, in *Barron's,* are:

- *Dow Jones Industrial Average.* Though this is the oldest stock index, it is really best used only as a comparative measure for investments in big, established companies. The Dow can rise even when most of the thirty stocks that make it up go down (and vice versa). This is because the higher-priced stocks in the index have a greater influence on the calculation of the index.
- *Standard & Poor's 500 Composite Stock Price Index.* The S&P 500 has a broader representation of company stocks than the Dow, but most of them are also large, well-known companies. Higher-priced stocks don't dominate in the calculation of this index, but it has

another bias. Companies with a great many shares outstanding selling at fairly high prices (such as IBM) have a major influence on how the index moves.

• *New York Stock Exchange Composite Index.* This is even broader than the S&P 500, covers about 1,600 stocks, and is calculated in much the same way as the S&P 500. It's a good benchmark for big-company stocks.

• *Wilshire 5000 Equity Index.* This takes in virtually every actively traded stock and is the broadest measure of overall market activity.

• *NASDAQ Composite Index.* This covers 4,700 or so actively traded over-the-counter issues. This is a good comparative measure for your holdings of smaller companies.

• *Value Line Composite Index.* This covers about 1,600 stocks (much the same as the New York Stock Exchange Composite Index), but in calculating the index, big-capitalization stocks do not dominate as they do in the other index. This is a good comparative measure for lower-priced stocks.

How to Buy Stocks Wisely

If, after reviewing the Investment Guides in Part Two of this book, you are in the market for individual stocks for your college fund, use the research services of a full-service securities firm to help you make decisions or do your own research and place orders through a discount broker. If you invest through a full-service firm, you should know something about its performance record in selecting stocks before you sign on. Ask for some comparisons, for instance, on how its stock recommendations over time have performed in relation to the overall market. Lipper Analytical Services ranks the performance of mutual-fund managers. You would want to work with a securities firm that performed above the five-year average for that group. *The Wall Street Journal* reports every quarter on the relative performance of the stock selections of major brokerage firms. Or you could ask for a comparison with the performance of other professional money managers.

Securities firms are often criticized for encouraging customers to buy stocks when an analyst makes a positive case for a company—but neglecting to inform customers when the outlook for the company sours. So, also ask what the firm's practice is on communicating negative information—and "sell" recommendations. *Ask to see some.*

One approach to making sure that your portfolio contains attractive stocks is the discipline used by PaineWebber's Focus List. The guiding rule is "Let profits run and limit losses."

The Focus List is created by a committee of PaineWebber strategists, senior-level brokers and branch managers. The committee reviews current "buy" and "attractive" rated stocks (by the firm's analysts) using fundamental, technical, and quantitative screens. This would include such elements as looking at the stock's current valuation, future potential, and recent trading patterns.

The ratings of "buy" and "attractive" refer to a system used by PaineWebber's fundamental analysts to rank stocks. Research departments at different firms may use a similar ranking system. Be sure to understand what the ratings represent.

1. "Buy" The stock is expected to outperform the market by more than 10% over the next twelve months and the timing and fundamentals are so strong that the analyst considers this an urgent recommendation.

2. "Attractive" The stock is also expected to outperform the market by more than 10%, but the buy recommendation is somewhat less urgent than for a #1 stock.

3. "Neutral" The stock is expected to perform about the same as the market over the next twelve months.

4. "Unattractive" The stock is expected to underperform the market by 10% over the next 12 months.

5. "Sell" The company's fundamentals are poor and it is also expected to underperform the market by 10%.

PaineWebber removes a stock from its Focus List if it closes 15% below its high price (after adjusting for its usual rate of fluctuation) since it was included on the List.

Stocks might be deleted from the List entirely or its rating downgraded, too, if the analyst uncovers negative information.

PaineWebber's expectation is that a customer who follows its Focus List recommendations will avoid substantial losses and, at the same time, hold on to stocks that are in long-term rising trends through normal, temporary setbacks.

Appropriateness Guide

Early Planners: These are the prime candidates for stock or equity-fund investments. Select stocks for long-term holding—at least two years—or dollar-cost average fund share purchases. For individual stocks, use stop-loss orders (or follow recommendations of your securities firm) to preserve gains and limit losses.

Late Starters: Should be holding steady or paring down, not adding, stock or stock funds to the college fund.

Last-minute Savers: Stocks and stock funds are generally *not* appropriate especially if you have few other financial resources, because of the risk that shares will have to be sold during a down-market.

16

Real Estate, Real-estate Partnerships, and Investment Trusts: Long-term Wealth-builders

Real estate, in the form of a house or a condominium, is still most people's favorite investment—one that appreciates (hopefully) while you enjoy the use of it. These familiar forms of real-estate investment can play a major role in meeting college expenses—and the earlier you start planning for their maximum use, the more they can contribute to your college fund. The professional types of real-estate investment that you might consider for your college fund *must* be entered into while your child is young.

FAMILIAR PROPERTIES

First: The family home. If you own a well-appreciated property with a low mortgage, a home-equity loan around the time college expenses begin can fill in the difference between what's available from the college fund and what's needed. Interest paid on equity loans of up to $100,000 is fully deductible.

Next: Some real property that the family may own in addition—an inherited house that's rented out for income, a summer place, a rental apartment building, or shopping center bought as an investment.

Consider deeding a share of any income-producing real estate to a Minors Trust set up for your child, unless the property is also producing generous depreciation deductions for you. As explained in Chapter Three, $500 of that real-estate income could then be distributed from the trust to your child tax-free each year and the trust will pay only 15% tax on the next $5,000. Let your college fund benefit from the tax saving between what you would pay on that income and what you'd pay under this arrangement.

If you're considering taking back a promissory note from the buyer on a portion of the sale price for your home or any other property, you could also make a gift to your child's trust of, say, 10% or 20% of the promissory note. Then, 10% or 20% of the interest payments would be taxed at the trust's rate and not yours, further enhancing the college fund.

Be careful, of course, that gifts of shares in either the home or the promissory note do not exceed the $10,000 per year gift-tax exclusion for individuals or the $20,000 limit for couples. Tax savings aren't all you should think about either. Many states, and even some cities, levy a transfer tax when the title on real estate is changed. And sharing the ownership of a piece of property or a promissory note with a Minors Trust could wind up being an encumbrance.

If you own a property (even a parcel of land) that has appreciated in value and you plan to sell it eventually, deeding a share of the property over to your child or your child's trust well before the sale can also put dollars into your college fund rather than into the coffers of the IRS. The gain in value from your original cost to the selling price would then be taxed at the trust's rate or, after the child is age 14, at the child's tax rate rather than at yours.

If you plan to make a gift of appreciated property to your child, be sure to do it *before* you negotiate any sale—even before you begin any oral discussion with a potential buyer or list the property with a broker. You don't want to provide the IRS with any grounds for challenging the fact that your child owned the property at the time of sale and that the gains are taxable to her.

REAL-ESTATE LIMITED PARTNERSHIPS

You can also acquire income-producing property in various types of investment packages and use them as one of the engines of growth for your college fund. This is usually somewhat less familiar territory than the family estate.

Real-estate limited partnerships originated as tax shelters years ago, but successive tax reforms wiped out tax advantages as their prime feature. Now these partnerships are generally designed to produce current returns of 9% to 10% a year, some of it sheltered from taxes because of depreciation and mortgage-interest expense deductions. If the general manager of the partnership selects his properties wisely, you could also expect to have a handsome capital gain in seven or so years. That's about the time most such partnerships are ready to sell their holdings, distribute any gains to partners, and close down the partnership.

Obviously, the key to producing this kind of success is real-estate savvy in choosing properties and location. You really don't have much to go on to appraise this skill except the past performance of the general partners who will be running the partnership's real-estate holdings. Make sure, therefore, that you take the time to examine the complex partnership agreement to find out what that record is—and ask your broker or accountant to help you evaluate it. A good sign: The general partners have bought similar properties in the past. As to how well they did in producing profits for the investors in their former partnerships, use your Treasury-bond yardstick to figure that out. Since real estate is a fairly illiquid investment, their return should have been *at least three points over the long-term U.S. government bond rate during that time.*

You must feel very confident about taking a stake in one of these partnerships (the minimum investment ranges from $2,000 to $5,000), because in most circumstances you will receive your maximum return by sticking with the partnership until it's scheduled to wind down.

Appropriateness Guide

Real-estate partnerships are usually most suitable for *Early Planners* because of the seven-year stretch generally needed to realize maximum profits.

REAL-ESTATE INVESTMENT TRUSTS

Real-estate Investment Trusts (REITs, pronounced "reets") are also packages of income-producing properties, but REIT shares are sold on exchanges. They're roughly similar to closed-end equity funds and they, too, frequently trade at a discount to the value of their holdings.

REITs have typically yielded about 6% to 8% a year with a good portion of the dividend treated as a return of capital. The benefit: You can defer taxes on that part until you sell your shares.

Look closely at REITs with much higher yields. They could be very highly leveraged or invested in highly speculative properties. On the other hand, they could simply be selling at a deep-discount because of current market psychology and represent a longer-term investment opportunity.

Appropriateness Guide

REITs, unlike real-estate partnerships, are liquid because they are traded on exchanges. But you probably should plan to stick with such an investment for *at least three years, and preferably longer,* to benefit from the real-estate appreciation. So, REITs, too, are most appropriate for the new savings of *Early Planners.*

IV.
THE MEANS TO BE SUCCESSFUL

Use this section of the book to gain an understanding of the current trends in financial aid for college students and the way a family's capacity to pay is calculated.

17

Financial Aid and Other Boosts to Your College Fund

Your best efforts to build a college fund may still leave you short of being able to meet all your child's tuition bills. Don't automatically consider that particular school out of the question—even if it's a high-priced college. Apply for financial aid. The most selective schools are, by and large, the ones with the largest endowments and the oldest tradition of helping deserving students. A good number of top schools have an announced policy of conserving all their aid money only for students who meet their criteria for acceptance but can't meet the cost; they are publicly opposed to the concept of "non-need (merit) scholarships." Even if your family income is substantial and you think your chances of qualifying for aid are nil—apply! Many of the families currently applying for aid at Ivy League–level schools report incomes in the $70,000–$80,000 range, so you're likely to be in good company. Special factors may favor you, such as your age or the number of children you have going to college at the same time, and you could qualify for financial aid even with an income over $100,000.

Since so much of the financial-aid package available to a college student is now directly and indirectly related to government programs, it's impossible to know precisely what the situation will be by the time your child is ready for college. The demand for spots at the highest-ranked colleges continues to increase sharply and well ahead of the growth of their endowments. Dr. Frank Leana, of Howard Greene Associates in New York, who has counseled families for twenty years on college placements, says that as tuitions have zoomed, parents are willing to make major financial sacrifices to get their children into top schools, though they're less willing to pay higher tuitions at lower-regarded schools. Though the most selective schools have the most money, as long as their tuitions and applications continue to increase, you'd be safer to anticipate a change in financial-aid availability—it probably will be *harder* to get aid in the future than it is now.

The trend is certainly headed in that direction. The federal government's policy on aid to higher education has clearly moved away from grants and toward loans and tax-advantaged savings. The College Board estimates that annual borrowing for college in the U.S. is already approaching $15 billion. The latest survey of entering college freshmen (the class of 1992) by the American Council on Education and the Higher Education Research Institute revealed that the students were now relying far more on family contributions, savings, loans, and college-sponsored grants than on federal financial aid. In fact, only 16% of the freshmen reported receiving anything from the federal government's major aid program (Pell Grants)—less than half of the 32% who reported receiving the grants in 1980. Many of the state programs to support higher education are also designed to encourage family savings for college rather than to expand grants.

Loopholes in the financial-aid process are being tightened up, too. Parents now may be asked to provide financial-aid officials with access to the *actual* tax returns they filed with the IRS rather than simply submit photocopies of their returns. (Schools have referred applications with intentionally falsified information on income, assets, and the number of children in college to legal authorities for criminal prosecution.) The children of divorced couples who, in the past, often qualified for financial aid because the custodian parent (usually the mother) could show a very low income even though the other parent was wealthy, now may have to provide financial information on both parents to qualify for an aid program. Financial information is often requested, also, from a remarried parent's new spouse. Federal and state laws and many schools have tightened up their criteria for accepting a student's claim that he or she is "independent," or self-supporting. Even when a student satisfies these tougher new criteria, some schools still require the parents to supply financial data.

Keep these trends in mind as you review in this chapter a summary of the current practices on financial aid. Otherwise, you may draw a dangerous conclusion: that it is better to spend than to save because the less assets you have by the time your child is ready for college, the stronger your case for financial aid.

It is clearly true that current formulas for financial aid appear to favor spenders over savers. If your child worked every summer during high school and saved every cent in a bank account, a good portion of what he earned will have to be considered part of the family's contribution to college expenses. If, instead, he bought a car with his earnings, the family's contribution might be less. It is assets in the child's name and the parents' *earning power* (rather than their assets) that have the greatest impact on how much a family is expected to contribute. A family with two children and a pretax income of $60,000 a year could be expected to contribute $10,290 a year toward college expenses if it had $20,000 in assets and one child in school. If it had $80,000 in assets, its expected contribution would be only a maximum of $2,450 a year more. But another family with $80,000 in assets and an annual income of only $40,000 might be asked to contribute just $6,740 a year—$6,000 less. So, if you anticipate that your family income will be over $100,000 by the time your child is ready for school, you will probably have to come up with (or borrow) all, or a great portion, of his college expenses unless you will have several children in college at the same time.

WHO PROVIDES FINANCIAL AID

The total amount of aid your college-bound child may receive is called a "financial aid package," and it is put together by the financial-aid administrator at the school to which your child applies. The package could include federal and nonfederal aid, grants from the school itself, loans, and work-study opportunities arranged by the school.

Federal Government Sources

Grants

Virtually all federal government grants to undergraduates are awarded on the basis of need. Pell Grants (around $2,200 a year) do not have to be paid back. The U.S. Department of Education guarantees that each participating school receives enough money to pay the Pell Grants awarded to enrolled students. Schools also get a set amount of federal money for Supplemental Educational Opportunity Grants, which also do not have to be repaid and can reach up to $4,000 a year. The school uses its own discretion in distributing these Supplemental Grants—all on the basis of need. The federal government also supports the College Work-Study Program, which provides jobs for undergraduates who require financial aid. The school will set the hours of work and the amount each student can earn under this program. And a student's earnings from a college work-study program are not included in the formulas used to determine eligibility for aid in the following school year.

Federal-Backed Loans

The financial aid package may also include low-interest (5% a year) direct loans from the federal government. These Perkins Loans, as they are called, could be up to a total of $9,000 for undergraduate studies, with repayment starting about nine months after graduation.

You apply directly to banks and savings-and-loan associations for federally guaranteed loans to:

- *Students:* Stafford Student Loans (formerly known as Guaranteed Student Loans) are interest-free while the student is in college. Currently, interest is 8% during the first four years of repayment and 10% thereafter. These loans could provide $2,625 a year for the first and second years and $4,000 a year for the final two years of undergraduate study.
- *Parents:* Interest adjusted each year, currently 10.27%. Up to $20,000 can be borrowed under this program (called "PLUS") for each dependent child's college expenses and need is not a criterion.

More Information on Federal Aid and Loan Programs

Call 1-800-333-INFO, the Federal Student Aid Information Center, for information on applications and for a free copy of *The Student Guide: Five Federal Financial Aid Programs.*

School Sources

At many of the top-ranked private colleges, 75% to 90% of the aid money comes from the school's own financial resources rather than from federal programs. Though schools use their own judgment in deciding whom to accept, most of them use one of two standard financial-aid application forms (the school will tell you which one): The College Scholarship Service's Financial Aid Form (FAF) or the American College Testing Service's Family Financial Statement (FFS). Your child's high-school college counselor can usually provide the form. You fill it in and send it to a centralized processing service, which analyzes the income and asset information and arrives at a contribution figure for your family.

Estimated Capacity to Pay

In theory, what you are expected to contribute toward your child's education, if you qualify for financial aid, will be the same whether your child goes to a school with a $4,000 tuition, an $8,000 tuition, or a $12,000 tuition.

The formulas used to arrive at your capacity to pay *do not assume that you will be able to meet this expense out of current income.* The estimate of what you should be able to provide assumes a combination of savings, current earnings, and loans. Without advance savings, of course, much more will have to come out of current income and, possibly, loans.

Some judicious shifting of assets could result in strengthening your case for more aid. According to Kalman Chany, president of the Manhattan financial-aid consulting firm Campus Consultants Inc., the family's expected annual contribution toward college expenses drops by more than 5 cents for each dollar shaved off reportable assets.

Parents are allowed, for instance, to subtract from their assets a certain portion intended for retirement; the older the parents, the greater this "asset protection allowance." If the parents are between 40 and 44, the allowance is $32,900; at ages 50 and 54, it's $43,400; at ages 55 to 59, it's $51,000. The standard financial aid forms do not ask you to report the cash value of life-insurance policies you own, but some private colleges may ask you to disclose that information.

A far greater share of assets in your child's name (35%) than in your name (less than 6%) are expected to be contributed toward meeting college expenses. And 70% of the after-tax income your child earns in a prior year is expected to go toward college costs. (Most financial-aid packages assume the student will work during summer vacations.)

Kalman Chany recommends that parents who think income and asset shifting might make sense to improve their position to qualify for financial aid start planning when their child is in the tenth or eleventh grade—or even sooner. January of your child's junior year in high school is the beginning of the tax year that will determine your family's eligibility.

The table below gives you an approximate idea of what many colleges will expect your family to contribute to your child's education.

AVERAGE EXPECTED FAMILY CONTRIBUTION TO ANNUAL COLLEGE EXPENSES (ACCORDING TO GENERAL FINANCIAL-AID GUIDELINES FOR FAMILY WITH ONE CHILD IN COLLEGE)

1988 EARNED INCOME, BEFORE TAXES ($)	CONTRIBUTION, IN DOLLARS, WHEN SAVINGS AND OTHER ASSETS, MINUS MORTGAGE AND OTHER DEBT, TOTAL:			
	$20,000	$40,000	$60,000	$80,000
20,000				
FAMILY OF THREE	920	1,180	1,710	2,320
FAMILY OF FOUR	400	690	1,215	1,750
40,000				
FAMILY OF THREE	5,550	5,795	6,920	8,050
FAMILY OF FOUR	4,620	4,870	5,990	7,120
60,000				
FAMILY OF THREE	11,260	11,500	12,630	13,760
FAMILY OF FOUR	10,390	10,630	11,760	12,900

Reprinted with permission from *Meeting College Costs,* copyright © 1988 by College Entrance Examination Board, New York. Figures rounded by author.

Figuring Your "Need"

Your family's "need" for financial aid will be determined by the gap between your estimated capacity to pay and the total annual college expenses ahead of you at the school to which your child applies, including the cost of books, room and board, a basic personal expense allowance, and transportation expenses. "Just as you shouldn't simply

FINANCIAL-AID AWARDS TO ENTERING FRESHMEN FOR THE 1989 ACADEMIC YEAR AT THE FIFTY MOST EXPENSIVE COLLEGES

COLLEGE	1989 TUITION ($)	% OF 1987 FRESHMEN WHO APPLIED FOR AID	% OF AID APPLICANTS ASSISTED	AVERAGE AMOUNT AWARDED ($)	% OF AID THAT WAS OUTRIGHT GIFT
AMHERST	13,105	51	67	12,093	75
BARD	13,560	66	80	10,200	76
BARNARD	12,918	50	78	11,635	71
BATES	13,920	57	65	9,000	67
BENNINGTON	15,670	57	93	11,620	76
BOSTON UNIVERSITY	12,975	49	86	10,210	70
BOWDOIN	12,565	56	74	9,383	84
BRANDEIS	13,066	45	80	10,500	66
BROWN	13,759	44	75	10,988	68
BUCKNELL	12,460	45	77	8,296	62
CARLETON	12,485	69	67	8,546	67
COLBY	12,620	52	84	10,055	71
COLGATE	12,350	42	88	8,561	76
COLUMBIA COLLEGE	12,878	66	71	11,395	72
CONNECTICUT	12,800	41	86	10,000	75
CORNELL	13,140	56	70	9,310	69
DARTMOUTH	13,335	55	78	11,650	69
DREW	12,498	67	69	7,304	70
FRANKLIN AND MARSHALL	12,460	43	88	9,919	65
HAMILTON	12,750	51	79	10,380	78
HAMPSHIRE	13,845	60	77	10,445	71
HARVARD/ RADCLIFFE	13,665	60	84	10,604	72
HAVERFORD	12,770	53	65	9,519	83
HOBART	12,620	38	84	10,924	75
JOHNS HOPKINS	12,340	58	72	9,270	73
LEHIGH	12,450	45	76	8,819	73
MIT	13,400	75	80	10,952	70
MOUNT HOLYOKE	12,940	60	78	10,355	74
OBERLIN	12,926	64	79	9,834	69
PITZER	12,986	47	81	11,522	72
PRINCETON	13,380	53	78	10,689	71
RENSSELAER POLYTECHNIC	12,600	80	89	9,644	73
SARAH LAWRENCE	13,280	41	77	11,863	70
SKIDMORE	12,440	33	83	9,986	74
STANFORD	12,564	61	70	12,458	71
SWARTHMORE	13,230	68	77	12,576	78
TRINITY	13,200	70	48	6,907	N.A.
TUFTS	13,162	47	80	10,470	70
TULANE	12,730	40	95	12,400	77
UNIVERSITY OF CHICAGO	13,285	69	90	11,367	75

COLLEGE	1989 TUITION ($)	% OF 1987 FRESHMEN WHO APPLIED FOR AID	% OF AID APPLICANTS ASSISTED	AVERAGE AMOUNT AWARDED ($)	% OF AID THAT WAS OUTRIGHT GIFT
UNIVERSITY OF PENNSYLVANIA	12,750	55	82	11,184	70
UNIVERSITY OF SOUTHERN CALIFORNIA	12,466	59	93	9,716	77
VASSAR	12,490	56	81	10,641	75
WASHINGTON UNIVERSITY	12,574	51	91	11,152	71
WELLESLEY	12,580	59	79	9,914	68
WESLEYAN	13,325	95	72	6,960	60
WHEATON	12,370	63	82	5,042	68
WILLIAMS	12,975	55	70	10,166	75
WILLIAM SMITH	12,620	45	77	12,269	77
YALE	12,960	56	75	11,624	73

Data on financial aid from *Peterson's College Money Handbook 1989,* published by Peterson's Guides, Princeton, NJ. Data on tuition from *The College Cost Book, 1988–89,* copyright © 1988, College Entrance Examinations Board, New York. Both used with permission.

assume that you will be qualified for a certain amount of aid, you shouldn't simply assume that you won't qualify at all," counsels the College Scholarship Service of the College Board. "Financial aid doesn't just happen to people . . . you must apply for it."

The table above gives shows the proportion of entering freshman that applied for financial aid at the fifty most expensive colleges in the U.S., the percent who received aid, the value of that aid, and the portion of the aid that was an outright gift.

Non-need Scholarships

Though a number of the most selective colleges provide aid only on the basis of need, hundreds of schools, including most state universities, offer special awards to attract freshmen with particular talents and interests.

The easiest way to find out what's available is through annually updated books such as *Lovejoy's Guide to Financial Aid* or *Peterson's College Money Handbook. Don't Miss Out: The Ambitious Student's Guide to Financial Aid,* by Anna Leider, is also a useful and practical guide to the process of applying for aid.

When and How to Apply for Financial Aid

You will probably have to fill the financial-aid form you get from your child's college counselor sometime in January of the year your child will enter college. Make very sure you don't miss deadlines set by individual schools (some of which may have other financial-aid forms for you to fill out) or by state programs for special grants.

The centralized processing service to which you send your application will send results back both to you and to any schools you've indicated on the application. The processing organizations themselves do not award any financial aid.

When your child is accepted at a college, the school's financial-aid officer will let you know whether your family qualifies for financial aid and what its financial-aid "package" would be. The rule, according to financial-aid specialist Anna Leider, is "when awarding federal money, colleges give to the neediest of the able. When awarding their own funds, they select the ablest of the needy."

You have some latitude in negotiating with the school once you know the results. Your chances of greatly enhancing the package, however, are not very good unless your child's special talent spurs a college department head to support your request, or your family's financial condition suddenly worsens because one of the parents loses a job, is disabled, or dies. While selective schools have an informally coordinated system of not "bidding" for students by topping each other's financial-aid packages, you can try to bargain one school's aid package against another.

ADVANCE-PAYMENT PLANS

States and individual colleges have recently been attempting to ease the financial burden of escalating college tuitions by a variety of prepayment and savings plans. Even though these plans are not as flexible as building your own college fund, they are attractive to many anxious parents. An estimated $1 billion has already been committed to them.

Prepayment Plans

The idea of prepaying college tuition started when individual schools offered parents a way to contribute now in return for a guarantee that those contributions would cover future tuition at the school for their children. Obviously, such a plan significantly narrows your child's choice of school. Furthermore, these plans are more likely to be offered by schools that are apprehensive about future enrollments—which raises the question of what the status of the school will be by the time your young child is ready to apply for entrance. Even worse, one of the most widely publicized of these school plans turned out to be financially unsound and was eventually canceled.

But the legislatures of various states have taken up the idea—most of them to encourage enrollment in state institutions. By January 1989, nine states had passed guaranteed tuition bills: Florida, Indiana, Maine, Michigan, Missouri, Oklahoma, Tennessee, West Virginia, and Wyoming.

Many states follow Michigan's plan, which attracted $265 million from parents in three months for forty thousand tuition contracts when it was offered late in 1988. Parents of a kindergartner could choose, for instance, to contract for guaranteed payment of tuition and fees for four years at any Michigan four-year public college or university for their child with a $7,288 payment; those with eight-year-olds paid $7,904. The sums increase in relation to the child's age and decrease if the parents choose to buy limited benefits or to cover tuition at a community college. The Michigan plan sharply limits credits if they are to be used at colleges in another state and provides for refunds (never *less* than the amount a family committed to the plan) if the child wins a full scholarship, chooses to attend a private school, dies, or is disabled.

Another model plan pending in the Massachusetts legislature eliminates a typical disincentive of most state plans: It allows parents to use the credits in schools outside the state. But the "balkanization" of most existing state programs is a handicap to parents making plans to finance their child's education, according to Dr. Richard E. Anderson, head of the Forum for College Financing Alternatives at Teachers College, Columbia University: "To the extent the state lawmakers are unwilling to assist families for whom out-of-state attendance is desirable, these state programs are seriously flawed." If locking in tomorrow's tuition costs at something close to today's prices is attractive to you, you might find the CollegeSure CD (see page 88) a more flexible alternative.

State Savings Plans

By January 1989, fifteen states had passed legislation permitting the sale of state- and local-tax-free bonds designed for college savings plans. Six of the states had implemented the plans: Connecticut, Illinois, North Carolina, North Dakota, Oregon, and Washington. Most of these are simply zero bonds or general-obligation bonds that are being specially marketed to parents saving for their children's college educations. Some of the savings-bond plans still under consideration in various states, however, might offer special incentives if bond proceeds are used to pay tuitions to colleges in those states.

How to Invest in Advance-Payment Plans Wisely

Parents clearly find the idea of locking in tuition costs attractive, but many of these prepayment programs are inflexible and should be approached cautiously. Some of the key questions you should ask before making such an investment, according to the College Board, are:

- Can anyone in the family contribute to the plan? Is anybody specifically excluded?
- Are there restrictions that limit use of the funds to a particular group of schools?
- Is the yield from the plan guaranteed? Who guarantees it?
- Is the plan insured?
- Does the plan cover all college costs? Or only tuition?
- Are there age restrictions or time limits on use? Do proceeds have to be used within a certain number of years after high school?
- What are the refund conditions if the child is disabled, dies, or does not attend college?
- Does the family benefit if there is a surplus in investment results over the eventual college-cost level?
- Will benefits from the plan be taxable either at the federal or state level? (Each state plan is submitted to the IRS for an opinion.)

Be sure also to inquire how your participation in these programs affects your eligibility for financial aid.

18

Last Step. First Step.

The traditional theme at commencement ceremonies is that the last step out of college is the first step toward the rest of your life. Applying that message, once you find yourself consistently and successfully building your college fund, you may discover that you've developed a whole new set of skills to gain financial control of your future.

The day you write your last tuition check is an experience much like the day you make your last mortgage payment. Your earning capacity will probably still be at its peak but your "overhead" costs will suddenly go way down. A spending spree might in order. But that will also be the time to think hard about your own future—about early retirement, a career change, a move to another part of the country, giving yourself a chance to spend more time at a hobby or sport, to pursue an interest you've long postponed.

As an experienced saver and successful manager of your savings, you'll now be prepared to translate your personal dreams and aspirations into a plan. And you'll be able to make sure that plan is successful. This time, it's for you.

Appendix: Federal Reserve Banks in Your Area

NORTHEAST

In-person	Written
FRB Boston 600 Atlantic Ave. Boston, MA 617-973-3805 (recording) 617-973-3810	POB 2076 Boston, MA 02106
FRB Buffalo 160 Delaware Ave. Buffalo, NY 716-849-5046 (recording) 716-849-5030	POB 961 Buffalo, NY 14240
FRB New York 33 Liberty St. New York, NY 212-720-5823 (recording) 212-720-6619	Federal Reserve PO Station New York, NY 10045
FRB Philadelphia 10 Independence Mall Philadelphia, PA 215-574-6580 (recording) 212-720-6619	POB 90 Philadelphia, PA 19105

FRB Pittsburgh
717 Grant St.
Pittsburgh, PA
412-261-7988 (recording)
412-261-7863

POB 867
Pittsburgh, PA
15230

SOUTHEAST

In-person	Written
FRB Atlanta 104 Marietta St. NW Atlanta, GA 30303 404-521-8657 (recording) 404-521-8653	Same
FRB Baltimore 502 South Sharp St. Baltimore, MD 301-576-3300	POB 1378 Baltimore, MD 21203
FRB Birmingham 108 Fifth Avenue N Birmingham, AL 205-252-3141 x215 (recording) 205-252-3141 x268	POB 10447 Birmingham, AL 35283
FRB Charlotte 401 S. Tryon St. Charlotte, NC	POB 30248 Charlotte, NC 28230
FRB Jacksonville 800 W. Water St. Jacksonville, FL 904-632-1179	POB 2499 Jacksonville, FL 32231

FRB **Little Rock** 325 W. Capitol Ave. Little Rock, AR 501-372-5451 x273	POB 1261 Little Rock, AR 72203
FRB **Louisville** 410 S. Fifth St. Louisville, KY 502-568-9232 (recording) 502-568-9236 or 9238	POB 32710 Louisville, KY 40232
FRB **Memphis** 200 N. Main St. Memphis, TN 901-523-7171 x225, 641	POB 407 Memphis, TN 38101
FRB **Miami** 9100 N.W. Thirty-sixth St. Miami, FL 305-593-9923 (recording) 305-591-2065	POB 520847 Miami, FL 33152
FRB **Nashville** 301 Eighth Ave N Nashville, TN 37203 615-259-4006	Same
FRB **New Orleans** 525 St. Charles Ave. New Orleans, LA 504-522-1659 (recording) 504-586-1505 x293	POB 61630 New Orleans, LA 70161
FRB **Richmond** 701 E. Byrd St. Richmond, VA 804-697-8000	POB 27622 Richmond, VA 23261

MIDWEST

In-person	Written
FRB Chicago 230 S. La Salle St. Chicago, IL 312-786-1110 (recording)	POB 834 Chicago, IL 60690
FRB Cincinnati 150 E. Fourth St. Cincinnati, OH 513-721-4787 x334	POB 999 Cincinnati, OH 45201
FRB Cleveland 1455 E. Sixth St. Cleveland, OH 216-579-2490	POB 6387 Cleveland, OH 44101
FRB Detroit 160 W. Fort St. Detroit, MI 313-964-6153 (recording) 313-964-6157	POB 1059 Detroit, MI 48231
FRB Kansas City 925 Grand Ave. Kansas City, MO 816-881-2767 (recording) 816-881-2409	POB 440 Kansas City, MO 64198
FRB Minneapolis 250 Marquette Ave. Minneapolis, MN 55480 612-340-2075	Same

FRB Omaha 2201 Farnam St. Omaha, NE 68102 402-221-5638 (recording) 405-270-8652	Same
FRB St. Louis 411 Locust St. St. Louis, MO 314-444-8602 (recording) 206-442-1652	POB 14915 St. Louis, MO 63178

SOUTHWEST

In-person	Written
FRB Dallas 400 S. Akard St. Dallas, TX 214-651-6362	Security Station K 400 S. Akard St. Dallas, TX 75222
FRB San Antonio 126 E. Nueva St. San Antonio, TX 512-224-2141 x311 (recording) 512-224-2141 x303, 305	POB 1471 San Antonio, TX 78295
FRB Houston 1701 San Jacinto St. Houston, TX 713-659-4433	POB 2578 Houston, TX 77001
FRB Oklahoma City 226 Dean A. McGee Ave. Oklahoma City, OK 405-270-8660 (recording) 405-270-8652	POB 25129 Oklahoma City, OK 93125

WEST

In-person	Written
FRB Denver 1020 16 St. Denver, CO 303-572-2475 (recording) 303-572-2470 or 2473	POB 5228 Terminal Annex Denver, CO 80217
FRB Los Angeles 950 S. Grand Ave. Los Angeles, CA 213-624-7398	POB 2077 Terminal Annex Los Angeles, CA 90051
FRB Portland 915 S.W. Stark St. Portland, OR 503-221-5931 (recording) 503-221-5932	POB 3436 Portland, OR 97208
FRB Salt Lake City 120 S. State St. Salt Lake City, UT 801-322-7911 (recording) 801-355-3131	POB 30780 Salt Lake City, UT 84130
FRB San Francisco 101 Market St. San Francisco, CA 415-882-9798 (recording) 415-974-2330	POB 7702 San Francisco, CA 94120
FRB Seattle 1015 Second Ave. Seattle, WA 206-442-1650 (recording) 415-974-2330	Securities Services POB 3567 Terminal Annex Seattle, WA 98124

U.S. TREASURY, WASHINGTON, D.C.

In-person

Bureau of Public Debt
Securities Transactions
1300 C St. SW
Washington, DC
202-287-4113

Device for the hearing impaired:

202-287-4097

Written

Inquiries:
Bureau of Public Debt
Customer Services
300 13 St. SW
Washington, DC
20239-0001

Tenders to purchase:
Bureau of Public Debt
Department N
Washington, DC
20239-1500

Index

S

T

U

V

W

ABOUT THE AUTHOR

Marion Buhagiar has been a business and financial journalist and editor for thirty years. In January of this year, she wrote her last tuition check, having financed her daughter's education through a top Manhattan prep school and an Ivy league college without loans or financial aid.

As a *Time* magazine business reporter, Ms. Buhagiar contributed to several major cover stories on business and economics. She was then a writer, associate editor and director of story development for *Fortune* magazine for many years. She joined Boardroom Inc. in the mid-1970s to create and manage a new business-book operation, became top editor of the business newsletter *Boardroom Reports,* and helped create several other financial, tax, and technology newsletters.

In the mid-1980s, Ms. Buhagiar co-founded Expert Connections, the New York-based firm of marketing communications specialists that she now heads. The firm provides editorial, research, design, and survey services to corporations, publishers, and investment and other professional firms.

Fill out and send in the coupon on the back of this page for

PaineWebber's Personal Savings Plan
to Build a College Fund for Your Child

You will receive:

1. A projection of what it will cost you to send one or two of your children as an undergraduate to a particular school that you name—or to a general type of school, such as a private college in the Northeast.

2. Four savings plans that show you, year by year, how you can build the college fund you need to get one or two of your children through a top-notch four-year college *debt-free.*

The report is personalized—for *your* child or children, for the type or even the particular school *you* pick. Use the *PaineWebber Personal Savings Plan to Build a College Fund for Your Child* to set your goals now. Keep referring to it in the years ahead as a guide to where you are headed.

Fill in the information on the coupon on the back of this page.

Simply put the coupon in an envelope (no note is necessary) with your check or money order for $4 for each set of four savings plans ($5 if you name a specific school) made out to "Computing Independence." Send it to:

Computing Independence
POB 2031
New York, NY 10011

Please send me the *PaineWebber Personal Savings Plans to Build a College Fund* for my child or two children

Name ______________________________

Age January 1989 ______________________________

Name ______________________________

Age January 1989 ______________________________

I would like a year-by-year savings plan that would enable me to finance my child(ren)'s education at (select *one*):

One of the fifty most selective colleges in the U.S. __________

One of the top state universities __________

A four-year private college in

New England __________

Middle Atlantic __________

Southeast __________

Midwest __________

Southwest __________

West __________

This particular college (write name) ______________________________

(Enclose $5 if you write in a particular college, or $4 for any of the other choices. If you want four personalized savings plans for *more than one* school, enclose $4 for each school choice.)

Name ______________________________

Address ______________________________

City/State ____________________ Zip Code __________

Phone ______________________________

Cut out this coupon carefully. Enclose it with a check for $4 for each set of four savings plans ($5 if you write in a particular college) made out to "Computing Independence." No note is necessary.

Mail to: Computing Independence
POB 2031
New York, NY
10011

PaineWebber College Fund Sweepstakes

OFFICIAL ENTRY FORM

To enter, fill in the information below and return it to:
PAINEWEBBER COLLEGE FUND SWEEPSTAKES
The Putnam Publishing Group, Dept. JL
200 Madison Avenue
New York, N.Y. 10016

No purchase necessary. Void where prohibited by law. For complete rules, see below.

Name ______________________________

Address ______________________________

City/State ______________ Zip ______________

Telephone ______________________________

Mail this entry form *or* a plain 3″ × 5″ piece of paper with the required information, to be received no later than December 31, 1989.

WINNER WILL RECEIVE: A CollegeSure^{SM} CD from PaineWebber worth between $12,000 and $16,000 depending on the age of the named beneficiary when the prize is awarded. The CollegeSure^{SM} CD will earn interest at a rate directly linked to increases in the cost of a college education. The CollegeSure^{SM} CD is fully FDIC Insured, up to the maximum $100,000 limit per depositor allowed by law. Full details will be provided for the winner.

OFFICIAL RULES

1. On an official entry form or a 3″ × 5″ piece of paper, hand-print your name, address and telephone number and mail your entry in a hand-addressed envelope (#10) to PaineWebber College Fund Sweepstakes, The Putnam Publishing Group, Dept. JL, 200 Madison Avenue, New York, N.Y. 10016. *Only one entry per person.*

2. Entries must be received no later than December 31, 1989. Not responsible for misdirected or lost mail.

3. The winner will be determined in a random drawing from among all eligible entries held on or about January 15, 1990. The winner will be notified by mail no later than January 31, 1990. The odds of winning depend upon the number of entries received.

4. The sweepstakes is open to all U.S. and Canadian (excluding Quebec) residents. If a resident of Canada is selected in the drawing, he or she will be required to correctly answer a skill question to claim the prize. *No purchase necessary.* Void where prohibited by law. Employees and their families of PaineWebber; The Putnam Berkley Group, Inc.; MCA, Inc., their respective affiliates, retailers, distributors, advertising, promotion and production agencies are not eligible.

5. Taxes on the CollegeSure CD are the sole responsibility of the prize-winner, who may be required to sign and return a statement of eligibility within 14 days of notification. The name and likeness of the winner may be used for promotional purposes.

6. The prize-winner will be required to name a beneficiary for the College-Sure CD at the time the prize is awarded. A prize won by a minor will be awarded to his/her parent or legal guardian. The beneficiary must be a living child between the ages of 0 and 18. All terms and conditions of PaineWebber's CollegeSure CD will apply. The prize is nontransferable and nonredeemable for cash except as provided by the terms of the CD.

7. For the name of the prize-winner (available after January 31, 1990), send a stamped, self-addressed envelope to PAINEWEBBER COLLEGE FUND SWEEPSTAKES, The Putnam Publishing Group, Dept. JL, 200 Madison Avenue, New York, N.Y. 10016.